DEDICATION

INTRODUCTION

CHAPTER 1: UNDERSTANDING HOMELESSNESS: CAUSES, DYNAMICS, AND POPULATIONS

CHAPTER 2: TECHNOLOGICAL INNOVATIONS AND THEIR ROLE

CHAPTER 3: INNOVATIVE APPROACHES TO ENDING HOMELESSNESS

CHAPTER 4: COLLABORATIVE PARTNERSHIPS AND COMMUNITY ENGAGEMENT

CHAPTER 5: POLICY AND LEGAL FRAMEWORKS FOR HOMELESSNESS ERADICATION

CHAPTER 6: HOMELESSNESS PREVENTION AND EARLY INTERVENTION STRATEGIES

CHAPTER 7: HOMELESSNESS AND SOCIAL JUSTICE

CHAPTER 8: RESEARCH TOPICS

CHAPTER 9: THE PATH FORWARD

CHAPTER 10: CONCLUSION

REFERENCES

Dedication

To every individual who has felt the weight of a world
without walls,
To those who have known the stark loneliness of an
unyielding street,
Yet have carried on with unwavering spirit and undying hope.

To the unsung heroes, the tireless advocates and volunteers,
Who step forward every day, moving mountains with their
dedication,
Rekindling faith, sparking change, and proving that kindness
can indeed transform lives.

To the communities that rally together, embracing the power
of unity, compassion, and resilience,
Building bridges, breaking barriers, and lighting up the dark
corners of our society.

To the scholars, the researchers, the policy makers,
Who relentlessly seek solutions, challenging the status quo
and crafting pathways to a better tomorrow.

And to the future generations—our hope, our promise—
May you inherit a world where empathy reigns and where
every soul, no matter their journey, has a warm place to call
home.

This work is a testament to our collective dreams, struggles,
and hopes. May it inspire, challenge, and awaken.

Introduction

In the vast tapestry of human civilization, woven with tales of triumphs, discoveries, and advancements, there exist threads of sorrow, neglect, and injustice. One such thread, stark in its visibility yet often overlooked, is the issue of homelessness. It's a phenomenon that transcends borders, cultures, and economic structures, serving as a poignant reminder of the disparities and challenges still rampant in our society.

From Streets to Solutions: Innovating Against Homelessness is not just a book; it's a call to action, an invitation to delve deep into the labyrinth of homelessness, and, most importantly, a beacon of hope. Through its pages, we embark on a journey to understand the myriad faces of homelessness, its root causes, and the multi-dimensional challenges it presents.

Why does homelessness persist in a world bursting with technological advancements and unprecedented wealth? How do structural, economic, and personal factors collide, pushing individuals and families into the abyss of homelessness? These are just some of the critical questions we tackle as we navigate through the complexities of the issue.

But knowledge alone, while powerful, is insufficient. Thus, this book goes beyond just understanding the problem. It uncovers innovative approaches and strategies employed by communities worldwide to address homelessness, showcases the potential of technology in this fight, and underscores the importance of collaboration and community engagement.

We will also delve into the intersectionality of homelessness, examining how it intertwines with other social issues like mental health, substance abuse, and systemic poverty. In doing so, we illuminate the intricate web of challenges that many face, emphasizing the need for comprehensive solutions.

To every reader holding this book, know that you are not just embarking on a quest for knowledge but are also becoming a part of a global conversation—a conversation about equity, dignity, and the inherent right of every individual to have a safe place to call home.

As we journey from streets to solutions, may this book challenge your perceptions, ignite your passion, and propel you to be a catalyst for change in whatever capacity you can. Because in the end, it's not just about houses and roofs; it's about homes, hearts, and hope.

Homelessness, often perceived as a mere absence of shelter, is a multidimensional issue that strikes at the very core of societal well-being, human dignity, and our collective conscience.

The very existence of homelessness in our modern world, rife with advancements, is both a paradox and a challenge. From Streets to Solutions: Innovating Against Homelessness seeks to dissect this paradox, unraveling its many layers, while simultaneously presenting pathways to confront and alleviate it.

In our first chapter, we will delve deep into the intricate web of causes leading to homelessness. By understanding the structural, economic, social, and personal triggers, we can begin to appreciate the scale and depth of the challenge. Specific populations, like veterans and youth, are given dedicated focus, emphasizing the unique struggles they face.

Technological Innovations then emerge as a beacon of hope in the second chapter. In an age where data reigns supreme, we explore how big data, artificial intelligence, and other tech-driven tools can be harnessed to address and potentially prevent homelessness.

Our third chapter shines a spotlight on the innovative strategies and models being employed across the globe. The housing-first models, the role of supportive housing, and the transformational impact of wraparound services are dissected, offering insights into what's working and what's not.

As we transition to Collaborative Partnerships and Community Engagement in the fourth chapter, the emphasis is on unity. Real change demands a collective effort. Through heartening stories and case studies, we demonstrate the power of collaboration between government agencies, NGOs, businesses, and the homeless community itself.

Our journey then steers towards the legal and policy frameworks in the fifth chapter. Policies, when effective, can serve as powerful tools for change. We evaluate the existing frameworks, their gaps, and the urgent need for reform while also proposing evidence-based recommendations for future initiatives.

Recognizing that prevention is always better than cure, the sixth chapter focuses on early intervention strategies. From education to rapid rehousing, we scrutinize the various measures in place to prevent individuals from slipping into homelessness.

Homelessness isn't just an economic or social issue; it's also a profound matter of Social Justice. Chapter seven delves into the impact of homelessness on marginalized communities, the systemic inequities at play, and the vital role of advocacy in bridging these gaps.

Our eighth chapter on Research Topics is aimed at scholars and policymakers. Here, we delve into the leading edge of research, identifying emerging trends, methodologies, and gaps that need addressing.

The Path Forward chapter offers a visionary outlook. Drawing on insights from previous chapters, it serves as a roadmap for the future, emphasizing the ethical, sustainable, and human-centric innovations required to truly make a difference.

As you journey through these pages, remember: Each chapter, each insight, and each story are a steppingstone towards a world where homelessness is a thing of the past. It's a vision we can collectively achieve, one solution at a time.

Chapter 1: Understanding Homelessness: Causes, Dynamics, and Populations

Homelessness, a complex and multifaceted issue, affects millions of people worldwide, transcending borders, cultures, and economic systems. Its presence in both developing and developed nations underscores its universal nature, reminding us that, irrespective of a nation's prosperity, segments of the population remain marginalized, often living on the fringes of society.

To fully grasp the depths of homelessness and to discern a path toward its alleviation, one must first navigate its myriad causes and dynamics. This chapter sets out to accomplish just that by delving deep into the structural, economic, and social factors that lead to homelessness.

It is critical to understand that homelessness doesn't arise from a vacuum; it is an outcome—often the result of intricate interactions between societal frameworks, economic systems, and individual circumstances.

The chapter sheds light on personal triggers, such as mental health issues, trauma, and substance abuse, that often exacerbate an individual's susceptibility to homelessness. But while these triggers are critical, it would be an oversimplification to consider them in isolation. Interwoven with these individual factors are larger societal and economic dynamics. For instance, why do certain demographics—like veterans, youth, and families, or those grappling with mental health challenges - find themselves disproportionately represented among the homeless population? These questions require us to go beyond personal struggles and examine structural issues.

This chapter tackles a rather uncomfortable paradox:

How rapid economic growth, often celebrated as a hallmark of societal advancement, can simultaneously perpetuate and exacerbate homelessness.

This raises poignant questions about the nature of our growth models and the price some pay for such progress. By the end of this chapter, readers will have gained a comprehensive understanding of the multilayered and intertwined factors leading to homelessness, thereby establishing a robust foundation for the subsequent discussions and proposed solutions in the chapters to follow.

Structural, Economic, and Social Factors Behind Homelessness

Homelessness, at its core, is often deeply embedded within societal structures. A nuanced understanding of homelessness necessitates examining it through the lenses of structural, economic, and social dimensions.

Structural Factors

The built environment, urban planning, housing policies, and accessibility to essential services play crucial roles in homelessness. Cities with insufficient affordable housing often experience high rates of homelessness. Zoning laws that prioritize commercial developments or high-end residential properties over affordable housing options compound the crisis. Another structural aspect is the lack of adequate public facilities like shelters, whose capacity often falls dramatically short of the actual demand, especially during extreme weather conditions.

Economic Factors

Economic dynamics are intertwined with homelessness in myriad ways. Economic downturns, job losses, and a rising cost of living without proportional wage growth can swiftly push vulnerable populations into homelessness. Furthermore, gaps in social safety nets mean that a single financial setback—a medical emergency or unexpected job loss—can set individuals or families on a trajectory towards homelessness. The gentrification of neighborhoods, which might seem like economic progress on the surface, often displaces long-term residents, pushing them into instability.

Social Factors

Societal norms, stigmas, and systems of discrimination play significant roles in homelessness.

Marginalized groups, including racial and ethnic minorities, LGBTQ+ individuals, and immigrants, often face systemic barriers to housing, employment, and social services.

Additionally, societal stigma associated with homelessness can perpetuate the cycle, making it harder for individuals to find jobs or access services due to prejudice and discrimination. Family breakdowns, resulting from conflicts, abuse, or ostracization, can also push individuals, especially youth, into homelessness.

Understanding these structural, economic, and social determinants is critical in grasping the multifaceted nature of homelessness. It moves the discourse away from a simplistic narrative that places blame solely on individual circumstances and redirects attention to the broader societal and economic structures. Addressing homelessness, therefore, isn't merely about providing immediate shelter but requires a rethinking and restructuring of these larger systems.

To grapple with the intricacies of homelessness, it's essential to peel back the layers, to delve beneath the surface narratives and understand the deeper systemic underpinnings that shape this crisis.

While we've outlined the broader structural, economic, and social factors, it's time to understand the nuances and interconnectedness of these determinants.

The Reinforcing Cycle of Structural Inequities

The intricate web of structural determinants, in many cases, functions as a self-perpetuating machinery, where one gear feeds into the next, thereby exacerbating societal imbalances. Delve deeper into the housing crisis, and one observes that the absence of affordable housing is not a mere byproduct of insufficient policy measures. It's an intricate outcome of myriad interconnected systemic factors.

At the heart of this is the land valuation system. Urban areas, often seen as epicenters of growth and opportunity, are driven by property markets that value land based on its highest and best use. This paradigm, while financially lucrative, inadvertently prioritizes high-end developments, often sidelining the pressing need for affordable housing. The consequence? A real estate market that skews towards luxury condominiums, upscale malls, and office spaces, often at the expense of affordable residential projects.

Property taxes further contribute to this reinforcing cycle. Municipalities often derive substantial revenue from these taxes, and as property values rise, so does the revenue. This monetary influx, on the surface, might seem beneficial. However, it sets a dangerous precedent. City administrations can become heavily reliant on such high-end real estate contributions, making them less inclined to disrupt the status quo with affordable housing initiatives. The urban landscape, consequently, becomes increasingly inaccessible to those with limited means.

Investment priorities play a significant role as well. The allure of high returns from luxury developments often diverts both public and private investments away from projects that cater to lower-income groups. Such investment trends, driven by profit motives, further shrink the availability of affordable housing units in city centers, pushing lower-income families to the peripheries or into unstable housing conditions.

As these families are pushed out, they often find themselves distanced from essential services, job opportunities, and community networks. This geographical displacement does more than just rob them of a stable shelter; it jeopardizes their socio-economic mobility, creating a domino effect where lack of housing spirals into joblessness, reduced access to education, and diminished overall well-being.

The structural determinants of homelessness are not just linear but cyclical. They feed into each other, creating a vortex that pulls vulnerable populations deeper into the abyss of instability. To truly address homelessness, it is paramount to not only acknowledge these reinforcing cycles but to actively dismantle them.

The Mirage of Economic Prosperity

In the tapestry of economic discourse, the narrative of growth and prosperity often takes center stage. Skyrocketing stock markets, burgeoning industries, and rising GDPs are heralded as symbols of national success. And understandably so; for such indicators, on the surface, spell progress. But lurking beneath this shimmering facade is a more nuanced story, one that speaks to the disparities of how this prosperity is shared and to whom it ultimately accrues.

An economy in overdrive can paint a picture of universal betterment, but the colors used to craft this image are often selective. The fruits of rapid economic development, while abundant, don't necessarily fall from the tree in an even spread. Instead, they sometimes cluster in specific pockets, leading to an uneven distribution of wealth. As the upper echelons amass even greater fortunes, those at the bottom find their piece of the pie shrinking. This economic dichotomy, where wealth accumulates at the top while stagnating or even declining at the base, further entrenches socio-economic divisions.

Adding to this complexity is the contemporary job market landscape. The modern era, with its embrace of digital platforms and flexible work models, has given rise to the "gig economy." On the one hand, platforms like ride-sharing apps, freelance marketplaces, and short-term rental services have democratized employment, offering opportunities to many who might have previously been sidelined. However, the flip side reveals a murkier picture. These gigs, while plentiful, often come without the traditional safety nets of permanent employment. Health benefits, paid leave, job security, and pensions become luxuries rather than givens.

For those navigating the tumultuous waters of the gig economy, life can be a perpetual tightrope walk. The ebb and flow of demand can lead to fluctuating incomes, making financial planning a challenge. Without the cushion of benefits or the assurance of long-term employment, many individuals find themselves a single crisis away from economic ruin. An unexpected medical bill, a car breakdown, or even a global pandemic can swiftly push them from a state of precarious stability to the precipice of homelessness.

While economic prosperity is undoubtedly desirable, it isn't a silver bullet. Its benefits, if not channeled equitably, can create illusions of universal upliftment, masking the undercurrents of disparity. To truly harness the power of economic growth, it becomes imperative to ensure that its winds lift all sails, not just those of the most affluent ships.

Social Factors Beyond Stigma

Social determinants are not just about overt discrimination or societal norms. There's a subtler, more insidious side. Consider the systemic barriers in education that hinder upward mobility for marginalized groups or the criminal justice system that disproportionately affects certain communities, leading to a cycle of incarceration and homelessness.

Diving into the vast ocean of social determinants affecting homelessness, we find layers of intricacies that often remain overshadowed by more apparent challenges. While stigma and overt discrimination undeniably play their roles in perpetuating homelessness, deeper down, there exists a matrix of systemic factors that work silently, yet persistently, to reinforce societal divides.

Education, long hailed as the great equalizer, holds within its fold disparities that are both profound and pervasive. Many marginalized communities, facing a lack of access to quality education, find themselves ensnared in a quagmire where their potential remains unrealized. It's not just about insufficient school infrastructures or outdated curricula; it's about the inherent biases in educational policies, the absence of culturally inclusive content, and the socioeconomic barriers that preclude consistent school attendance. These nuances ensure that the promise of education as a passport to upward mobility remains, for many, an unfulfilled dream.

The tendrils of the criminal justice system weave another tale of systemic imbalance. While laws are often touted as being blind, their application reveals patterns of disparity. Certain communities, especially those already marginalized by race, economic status, or past histories, find themselves under the unrelenting gaze of law enforcement more frequently than others. This heightened scrutiny, combined with pre-existing biases, results in a disproportionate representation of these communities within the justice system. Once inside this cycle, the prospects become grim. With a criminal record, reintegration into society becomes a Herculean task. Job opportunities shrink, societal trust wanes, and the doors to stable housing often remain closed. This nexus between incarceration and homelessness isn't coincidental but is a byproduct of the deeply entrenched inequalities within the justice apparatus.

In shedding light on these subtler determinants, it becomes evident that the fight against homelessness is not merely about providing shelters or resources. It's about dismantling the deeply rooted structures that perpetuate disparity. It's about ensuring that each societal system, be it education or justice, operates with equity at its core, offering everyone an equal shot at stability and prosperity.

Understanding these complexities demands a paradigm shift in the discourse on homelessness. It necessitates acknowledging that homelessness is not just an issue to be tackled on the streets but within the very systems and institutions that structure our society. It's a call for introspection, for societies to look within their policies, economies, and social fabric, identifying and rectifying the deep-rooted systems that perpetuate homelessness. Only by addressing these foundational issues can we hope to craft sustainable, long-term solutions.

Personal Triggers: Mental Health, Trauma, and Substance Abuse

While structural, economic, and social determinants provide a macroscopic view of homelessness, diving into personal triggers helps illuminate the individual journeys and challenges that many experiencing homelessness face.

Mental health disorders, often stigmatized and misunderstood, can be both a cause and a consequence of homelessness. Conditions like depression, bipolar disorder, or schizophrenia can interfere with one's ability to secure stable employment, maintain relationships, or even carry out daily tasks. Conversely, the harsh realities of living without a home can exacerbate pre-existing mental health conditions or even give rise to new ones. The streets, with their inherent unpredictability and lack of safety, can be particularly traumatizing for those with mental health challenges, creating a feedback loop that makes escaping homelessness even more challenging.

Trauma, especially childhood trauma or adverse childhood experiences (ACEs), are intricately linked to homelessness.

Experiences of physical or sexual abuse, neglect, witnessing domestic violence, or growing up in a household with substance abuse can have long-lasting repercussions. These traumatic events can affect emotional regulation, trust in others, and even cognitive development. For many, the scars of trauma manifest in adulthood as struggles with relationships, employment, or mental health, all of which can be pathways to homelessness. Moreover, once on the streets, individuals are often exposed to further trauma, be it through violence, exploitation, or the sheer stress of survival, compounding their vulnerabilities.

Substance abuse, too, has a complex relationship with homelessness.

For some, addiction might be the precipitating factor leading to a loss of housing, while for others, the stresses of homelessness might lead to substance use as a coping mechanism. The societal view of addiction often oscillates between criminalizing and medicalizing it. However, seeing substance abuse through a compassionate lens, understanding its roots in trauma, mental health, or systemic inequalities, is crucial. The streets are seldom conducive to recovery; without stable housing, access to detox or rehabilitation becomes challenging, and relapses are frequent.

Personal triggers like mental health challenges, trauma, and substance abuse do not exist in isolation. They are often intertwined with, and exacerbated by, the broader systemic factors discussed earlier. Addressing these personal triggers, therefore, requires not only immediate medical or therapeutic interventions but also a holistic approach that considers the interplay of individual vulnerabilities with societal structures.

Dissecting Homeless Demographics: Veterans, Youth, Families, and Mental Health Challenges

When we think of homelessness, often a singular image or stereotype comes to mind. However, homelessness is not a monolithic experience; it affects various demographic groups differently, with each group facing unique challenges and requiring distinct interventions.

Veterans: The Silent Struggle Beyond the Battlefield

For many veterans, returning home from active duty marks the beginning of another battle, one less visible but equally challenging. The theaters of war, with their intense and often traumatic experiences, leave indelible marks on a soldier's psyche.

When the cacophony of war subsides, the echoes of these experiences persist, manifesting in various ways that make reintegration into civilian life a complex endeavor.

The physical injuries, some debilitating, are often the most conspicuous remnants of their service. These injuries can necessitate long-term care and rehabilitation, making routine tasks formidable and diminishing prospects of conventional employment. But beneath these tangible scars lie deeper, more elusive wounds. PTSD, a condition many veterans grapple with, is characterized by intrusive memories, heightened anxiety, and emotional numbness. These symptoms don't just affect the individual; they ripple outwards, straining relationships with loved ones and making social integration challenging.

Beyond the psychological realm, the transition from a regimented, purpose-driven life in the military to the comparatively unstructured civilian world can be disorienting. The skills honed on the battlefield, while invaluable, don't always have a direct correlation in the civilian job market. This disconnect, combined with the potential absence of up-to-date training in rapidly evolving industries, can make job hunting a daunting task. For those who do secure employment, the workplace culture, devoid of the camaraderie and shared purpose inherent in military units, can feel alienating.

The narratives and perceptions surrounding veterans can be polarized. On one end, they're venerated as heroes, and on the other, they might be mischaracterized based on the mental health challenges some face, leading to stigmatization. This dichotomy can create an environment where veterans feel both pedestalized and misunderstood, making genuine connections and community integration elusive.

In grappling with these multifaceted challenges, some veterans find themselves in precarious financial situations, leading to housing instability and, in unfortunate instances, homelessness. As society extends its gratitude to veterans for their service, it's imperative to recognize the intricate challenges they face upon returning home. Addressing their needs requires a multi-pronged approach: robust mental health support, tailored employment programs, and community education to bridge understanding and foster genuine reintegration.

Youth: Navigating a Precarious Path Amidst Homelessness

The vulnerabilities of youth, characterized by a period of personal development, self-discovery, and transition to adulthood, become amplified when juxtaposed against the backdrop of homelessness. Homeless youth, teetering on the cusp of adulthood, confront a set of challenges distinct from their adult counterparts, shaped by their tender age and the vulnerabilities it presents.

One of the profound tragedies of youth homelessness is its root causes. Apart from escaping abusive or dysfunctional households, a significant portion of these young individuals are thrust onto the streets due to factors entirely beyond their control.

The rejection faced by many LGBTQ+ youth from their families upon revealing their sexual orientation or gender identity is a heart-wrenching reality, leading to their disproportionate representation within the homeless youth demographic.

Once on the streets, their youth becomes both a shield and a target. On one hand, their adaptability and resilience might help them navigate the daily challenges of homelessness with a certain tenacity. Yet, simultaneously, their age makes them prime targets for nefarious elements. Exploitation isn't limited to labor or trafficking; it takes many forms, from coercive relationships where young individuals are manipulated due to their age and inexperience, to being lured into substance use, further entrapping them in the web of street life.

The fallout of homelessness on their education is another devastating blow. Without a stable environment to return to after school, keeping up with academic commitments becomes an uphill task. This disruption in their formative education years doesn't just translate to missed lessons but potentially truncates their dreams and aspirations. The long-term ramifications of an incomplete education, such as limited job prospects and sustained financial instability, further entrench them in the cycle of poverty.

The very societal structures meant to protect them often fail these youths. Shelters and services designed for adults might not cater to the unique needs of the younger demographic, sometimes even inadvertently placing them in harm's way.

What they require is a blend of immediate safety nets, like age-appropriate shelters, and long-term interventions, like mentorship programs and educational support, to chart a way out of homelessness.

In understanding the plight of homeless youths, it becomes evident that their battles aren't just against the immediate adversities of street life, but also against the long shadows these experiences cast on their futures. Addressing their challenges demands a compassionate, tailored approach that recognizes their potential and seeks to nurture it amidst adversity.

Veterans: Having served their country, many veterans return home carrying the burdens of war, both visible and invisible. Physical injuries, post-traumatic stress disorder (PTSD), and the challenge of reintegrating into civilian life can create a perfect storm, pushing some veterans into homelessness. Despite having specialized skills, many veterans find it difficult to secure civilian employment, and their experiences of combat can lead to mental health struggles that further isolate them from their communities.

Youth: Homeless youth are often an overlooked demographic, with their experiences markedly different from those of adults. Many might be fleeing abusive homes, while others may be ostracized due to their sexual orientation or gender identity. On the streets, they're at heightened risk of exploitation, trafficking, and addiction. Additionally, lacking a stable environment can disrupt their education, limiting their future opportunities and perpetuating a cycle of poverty and homelessness.

Families: The image of a homeless individual is often a solitary one, but homelessness affects families too. Economic hardships, sudden job losses, or domestic violence can render entire families homeless. Living without a home disrupts the children's education, impacts their nutrition, and introduces them to trauma early in life. Parents, meanwhile, face the Herculean task of protecting their children while navigating the myriad challenges of homelessness.

Mental Health Challenges: Mental health and homelessness are deeply intertwined. The chaos and unpredictability of life on the streets can exacerbate mental health disorders. Conversely, those with untreated or undertreated mental health conditions might find themselves homeless due to the inability to maintain employment, strained relationships, or the societal stigma associated with mental illness. Within the homeless population, those with mental health challenges are often the most vulnerable, facing heightened risks of victimization, poor physical health, and premature death.

Families: Bonded in Adversity Amidst the Homelessness Quagmire

The collective heartbreak of families battling homelessness paints a poignant scene quite distinct from the singular journey of an individual. These families, enveloped in the cocoon of shared hardships, experience homelessness through a prism that magnifies both their vulnerabilities and their strength.

For families, especially those with children, the descent into homelessness often comes with a maelstrom of circumstances. It's not just about losing a physical shelter; it's about the disintegration of the sanctuary that nurtures growth, dreams, and memories. This shared adversity, be it precipitated by financial downturns, health crises, or escaping volatile domestic situations, often thrusts families into unfamiliar territories where the rules of survival are starkly different.

Children, who are by nature dependent on the stability of their environment for holistic growth, are the most affected. The streets and temporary shelters, with their unpredictable rhythms, can be a whirlwind of confusion and anxiety for young minds.

The formative experiences they should be having — playful interactions, school routines, and the joy of simple home comforts — are replaced by the daily uncertainties of life in homelessness. The effects on their academic progress and social interactions can reverberate through their lives, sometimes casting long shadows on their aspirations and self-worth.

Parents in these situations bear a weight that's both profound and heart-wrenching. The parental instinct to shield and provide is tested daily. The normalcy of bedtime stories, regular meals, and school preparations is swapped for the urgency of securing shelter, food, and safety. The emotional toll of seeing their children grapple with circumstances no child should endure can be overwhelming. The silent sacrifices they make, often prioritizing their children's needs over theirs, underscore the depth of their resilience and love.

Navigating services and seeking aid becomes a complex dance. Not all facilities cater to the unique dynamics of families, and splitting up can sometimes become a distressing reality. The need, therefore, is for a compassionate infrastructure that respects the integrity of these familial bonds, offering them a united pathway out of homelessness.

In the broader tapestry of homelessness, families stand out as poignant reminders that the issue isn't just an individual challenge but a societal one. Their journeys underscore the need for multifaceted interventions that recognize the interconnected needs of family members, weaving them into a cohesive approach to pull them out of the throes of homelessness together.

Mental Health Challenges: A Labyrinth Within Homelessness

In the intricate web of factors contributing to homelessness, mental health stands out as a particularly potent force, casting ripples that influence every aspect of an individual's experience on the streets. Beyond the already challenging realities of homelessness, those grappling with mental health disorders find themselves navigating an even more complex labyrinth, where the walls are shaped by both their internal struggles and external adversities.

For many, the very environment of homelessness — with its inherent instability, exposure to elements, and lack of privacy — can intensify existing mental health issues.

The constant vigilance required to find food, shelter, and safety, coupled with the isolation and often dehumanizing experiences on the streets, can further erode mental well-being. Episodes of anxiety, depression, or other disorders can become more frequent and severe, with the chaos outside resonating with the turmoil within.

It's crucial to understand that for a significant segment of this demographic, mental health challenges predate their homelessness. The spiral often starts with the onset or worsening of a mental health condition, which then cascades into a series of life-altering events. These might include the loss of a job, eviction due to erratic behaviors, or even the dissolution of familial and social ties. The stigma and misunderstandings surrounding mental illnesses compound these challenges, pushing individuals further to the peripheries of society.

Within the broader homeless community, those battling mental health challenges confront an additional set of vulnerabilities. Their conditions might make them less equipped to advocate for themselves or access available resources. This susceptibility exposes them to greater instances of exploitation, physical violence, and neglect. Their physical health, too, takes a disproportionate hit as they might prioritize their immediate survival over seeking medical or therapeutic interventions, leading to a convergence of mental and physical ailments.

The cycle becomes even more entrenched when societal systems fail to address the intersectionality of mental health and homelessness. Often, they fall through the cracks, with mental health facilities inadequately equipped to handle their housing needs and homeless shelters ill-prepared to offer mental health support.

Breaking this vicious cycle demands an integrated approach that goes beyond merely offering shelter. Holistic interventions, bridging medical, psychological, and social support, are crucial. The vision should be of systems that not only provide respite from the streets but also nurture the mind, recognizing the intertwined nature of housing and mental well-being.

Dissecting these demographics underscores the multifaceted nature of homelessness. While there are shared struggles — the lack of shelter, the daily fight for sustenance — each group brings to light specific challenges that necessitate targeted solutions. By understanding the unique needs and experiences of these demographics, society can better tailor interventions, ensuring that every individual, regardless of their background or circumstances, finds their way back to stability and dignity.

The Vicious Cycle: Economic Growth at the Expense of Stability

In the sprawling landscape of modern society, there's an overarching narrative that often goes unquestioned: the relentless pursuit of economic growth. Nations, cities, and communities are continually driven by the desire for expansion, modernization, and prosperity. However, beneath the glittering skyline of towering skyscrapers and the hum of bustling markets lies a stark reality that reveals a more intricate and paradoxical relationship between economic growth and stability.

The fervor for growth, while ushering in advancements, can also inadvertently prioritize the needs of capital over the well-being of individuals.

This dynamic is evident in the urban landscapes worldwide, where gleaming new developments might stand adjacent to dilapidated housing, or where rising rents spurred by gentrification push long-time residents into precarious living situations. The gravitational pull of economic centers attracts a multitude of individuals seeking better prospects, but not all find a foothold in this ever-shifting terrain.

Amidst this fervor, many individuals find themselves on the losing end of the bargain. Jobs that once offered stability become casualties of automation or shifts in industry preferences. Simultaneously, the cost of living — driven by speculative property markets and the influx of global capital — continues to rise, making basic necessities, particularly housing, increasingly unattainable for many. As cities and regions swell with opportunity, they simultaneously brew conditions where the very essence of stability, a home, eludes a significant segment of the population.

The kind of growth pursued can often be shortsighted, focusing on immediate gains rather than sustainable futures. Rapid urbanization without adequate planning for affordable housing or comprehensive social services leads to burgeoning slums and homelessness. Infrastructure might cater to the new corporate complexes, while neglecting the peripheral areas where many of the city's workers reside.

This cyclical dynamic raises profound questions about the very nature of growth and progress. Can economic growth truly be labeled as progress if it simultaneously destabilizes a significant portion of the populace? Is there a way to harmonize the scales of economic advancement and social stability, ensuring that the march of progress doesn't leave a trail of disenfranchised individuals in its wake?

Reimagining growth involves infusing empathy into economics. It beckons a shift from purely quantitative metrics, like GDP, to more holistic measures that account for well-being, equity, and sustainability. Crafting a future where economic dynamism and stability coexist requires a recalibration of priorities, ensuring that the quest for prosperity doesn't come at the cost of the most vulnerable.

By dissecting this intricate relationship, we can begin to chart a course that values both growth and stability, envisioning a world where economic progress uplifts all, rather than leaving many adrift in its turbulent wake.

Chapter 2: Technological Innovations and Their Role

In our rapidly evolving world, technology has emerged as a potent force, reshaping landscapes, redefining industries, and revolutionizing how we perceive and address age-old challenges. One such challenge, homelessness, has persisted across eras and geographies, presenting itself as a multifaceted issue that transcends simplistic solutions. Yet, with the dawn of the digital age, we stand at an unprecedented juncture where technological innovations hold the promise of shedding new light on this deeply entrenched societal problem.

This chapter delves into the transformative potential of technology in reimagining our approach to homelessness. From harnessing the vastness of big data to uncover patterns and insights in homelessness research, to leveraging the predictive prowess of artificial intelligence in devising prevention strategies and optimizing resource allocation — we are at the cusp of a paradigm shift. Yet, as with all powerful tools, technology brings with it a set of ethical dilemmas and challenges. The questions of privacy, ownership of data, and the imperative of ensuring digital literacy for all, emerge as critical considerations in this new frontier.

As we navigate the promise and complexities of this digital revolution, it becomes imperative to strike a balance. A balance where technology serves as an enabler, amplifying our efforts to combat homelessness, while ensuring that its deployment is responsible, inclusive, and anchored in the principles of equity and justice.

Let us then turn to the confluence of technology and the enduring challenge of homelessness, as we unpack the potential, the pitfalls, and the path forward in harnessing technological innovations for a more inclusive future.

The Promise of Big Data and Analytics in Homelessness Research

In the realm of today's data-driven world, the term 'big data' is more than a mere buzzword; it represents a seismic shift in how we gather, process, and interpret information. With every click, swipe, and interaction, vast amounts of data are generated, painting a detailed mosaic of human behavior, trends, and patterns.

When applied to the complex challenge of homelessness, big data and analytics offer transformative potential, providing unprecedented insights and refining our understanding of the issue.

Big data enables us to capture a holistic picture of homelessness. Traditional methods of data collection, like surveys and censuses, have their merits but often offer a snapshot in time, potentially missing the fluid dynamics of those moving in and out of homelessness. With big data, we can aggregate diverse sources, from social services databases to emergency room visits, painting a more comprehensive and real-time picture of homelessness's scope and nuances.

Advanced analytics can help identify previously unnoticed trends or correlations. For example, by analyzing rental market fluctuations alongside emergency shelter demand, researchers might discern patterns suggesting a relationship between housing costs and the onset of homelessness. Such insights can be invaluable in informing policy and intervention strategies.

Another promising avenue is the potential for predictive analytics. By analyzing data on individuals at risk of homelessness, algorithms can identify those most likely to become homeless in the near future. Such foresight can catalyze early intervention measures, ensuring resources are directed proactively rather than reactively.

The application of big data and analytics isn't solely about numbers and algorithms. At its heart, it's about people. With refined data, we can personalize interventions, understanding that each individual's journey into and out of homelessness is unique. Tailored support plans can be developed, ranging from mental health services to job training, ensuring a more targeted and effective approach.

However, while the potential of big data in homelessness research is immense, it's essential to approach it with sensitivity and caution.

The very nature of big data implies vastness, but within this vastness, the individual stories, the personal trials and tribulations, should not be lost.

Instead, they should be the driving force, reminding us that behind every data point is a human being with hopes, dreams, and the inherent right to dignity and shelter. As we delve deeper into this chapter, we will explore the intricate interplay of technology and humanity, and how, when wielded with care and empathy, big data and analytics can be formidable allies in our quest to understand and ultimately eradicate homelessness.

Within the vast oceans of data, every individual point carries with it the echoes of personal narratives, encompassing the aspirations, fears, and experiences of real people. These aren't just numbers or faceless statistics but stories of perseverance, resilience, and at times, despair. Such is the power and responsibility inherent in big data; it demands a lens of compassion and understanding, recognizing the profundity of life experiences encapsulated within.

As technology continues its relentless march forward, the juxtaposition of its cold precision with the warmth of human emotion presents a compelling paradox. It's a dynamic that underscores the essence of our journey through this chapter.

We are at a juncture where we have the tools to process vast amounts of data at speeds previously unimaginable. Yet, our challenge remains to always remember the individual lives behind those data sets. To ensure that our technological endeavors serve to amplify their voices, rather than drown them out.

Harnessing the power of big data requires more than just technical expertise; it necessitates a heart attuned to the myriad human stories it represents. When approached with this holistic perspective, the blend of technology and humanity can reveal insights and pathways previously hidden, guiding us toward a world where homelessness is not just understood better but is actively and empathetically addressed.

In an era where data drives decisions, the sheer volume of information at our fingertips can be both a boon and a bewilderment. Big data, with its vast repositories of information, has the potential to illuminate the darkest corners of societal issues. Yet, beneath the graphs, charts, and algorithms, lies the pulsating heartbeat of individual human experiences. These aren't mere numbers; they are lives, aspirations, setbacks, and triumphs.

To truly harness the potency of big data in understanding and addressing homelessness, we must approach it as more than just a computational challenge. Each data point reflects someone's journey, a mosaic of emotions, challenges, and potential. As we delve into the patterns and trends, it's crucial to maintain a delicate balance: the precision of technology with the empathy of humanity. Such a union ensures that the insights derived are both accurate and compassionate.

Consider, for example, the plight of a single mother navigating the maze of homelessness. Data might provide us with statistics on the number of single parents without stable housing or the average duration of their homeless spells. But to fully grasp her challenges, we must interpret this data in light of the broader societal structures. What barriers does she face in accessing childcare? How does the gig economy impact her ability to secure stable employment? How do cultural norms shape her experiences?

By synthesizing big data's vastness with a keen understanding of individual narratives, we can chart more holistic strategies. It's not just about identifying hotspots of homelessness or predicting future trends. It's about understanding the underlying forces at play, the systemic challenges, and the individual dreams.

In this convergence of technology and empathy, we find a potent tool. A tool that not only deciphers the intricacies of homelessness but also propels us to design interventions that resonate with the real needs and aspirations of those affected. This is big data with a conscience, steering us towards a future where our responses to homelessness are as technologically advanced as they are deeply human.

AI and Predictive Analysis: Prevention and Resource Allocation

Artificial Intelligence (AI), once the stuff of science fiction, has firmly rooted itself in the realities of today's world. It's revolutionizing fields from healthcare to finance, and its potential in addressing homelessness is just beginning to be realized. Among its many applications, predictive analysis stands out, offering a proactive approach to tackling the multifaceted issue of homelessness.

One of the most powerful abilities of AI lies in its capacity to analyze vast datasets quickly and identify patterns that might be too subtle for human analysts to notice. By drawing from diverse sources like medical records, employment histories, housing data, and more, AI can predict which individuals or families are at the highest risk of experiencing homelessness in the imminent future. With such knowledge, intervention can shift from being reactive — helping those already homeless — to proactive, preventing homelessness before it even begins.

This preemptive approach is not only more humane, ensuring individuals don't suffer the trauma of losing their homes, but it's also more cost-effective. Providing early support, be it in the form of financial assistance, counseling, or job training, can avert the more considerable costs associated with emergency shelters, healthcare, and law enforcement interactions often associated with homelessness.

AI's can also play a pivotal role in resource allocation. With a clear understanding of where the highest risks and needs lie, local governments and NGOs can more efficiently distribute their resources, ensuring that shelters, food programs, and other essential services are available where they are most needed.

AI can facilitate continuous learning and adaptation. As interventions are rolled out, AI systems can monitor their effectiveness in real-time, adjusting strategies based on the data. If a particular approach isn't yielding the desired results, systems can flag it for review, ensuring that efforts are always optimized.

However, with great power comes great responsibility. While AI offers transformative potential, its use raises ethical questions, particularly around privacy and consent. Using personal data for predictive analysis necessitates stringent safeguards to ensure that individuals' rights are not compromised. Furthermore, while AI can suggest courses of action based on data, human judgment and empathy must remain at the decision-making core, ensuring that strategies remain person-centered and respect the dignity of all involved.

The interweaving of technology and humanity has the promise to create a future where homelessness is not just a challenge of the past but a testament to our collective innovation and compassion. While the allure of technology, especially AI, is undeniably tantalizing, it's essential to tread with both curiosity and caution. The data AI consumes, interprets, and acts upon directly ties back to real individuals and communities. Each algorithm's prediction or recommendation has tangible effects on lives, underscoring the need for rigorous oversight and ethical considerations.

One of the foundational benefits of AI lies in its adaptability. With every piece of data processed, the systems learn, refine, and evolve, seeking ever more accurate and impactful outcomes. This dynamic nature means that our interventions can be continually honed, ensuring that our strategies remain not only effective but also relevant as societal conditions change.

The dynamic nature of AI also brings challenges. How do we ensure that the algorithms, in their quest for efficiency, don't inadvertently perpetuate societal biases? How can we maintain transparency in AI operations, allowing stakeholders, including those at risk of homelessness, to trust and understand the decisions being made on their behalf?

While AI offers a new frontier in our approach to addressing homelessness, it doesn't operate in a vacuum. It needs to be integrated seamlessly with existing systems — healthcare, housing, social services — to yield meaningful results. Collaboration across sectors will be paramount, ensuring that the insights gleaned from AI are actionable and lead to holistic solutions.

At the heart of all these considerations is the individual.

Technology's role is not to replace the human touch but to enhance and amplify it. It's a tool that, when used with empathy and respect, can illuminate paths forward that were previously obscured. Through a judicious blend of data-driven insights and human-centric approaches, we inch closer to a world where everyone has a place they can call home, and homelessness becomes a relic of a bygone era.

Special Highlight: Greater Change – Bridging Innovation and Compassion

In our journey through the multifaceted landscape of homelessness, it's imperative to spotlight solutions that capture the essence of innovation, humanity, and practicality. One such initiative that stands out is "Greater Change" from England.

Reimagining Altruism in the Digital Age

In a world transitioning to cashless transactions, street donations to the homeless have dwindled. Greater Change tapped into this paradigm shift, offering a solution that aligns with our modern habits. Using QR codes, the initiative allows passersby to scan and contribute digitally, ensuring that the spirit of giving isn't lost in our fast-paced, digital-first world.

Purpose-driven Contributions

Beyond the method of giving, what truly distinguishes Greater Change is its purpose-driven approach. Every individual enrolled has a defined savings goal—be it securing a rental deposit, procuring identification, or enrolling in training courses. This specificity not only provides transparency to the donor but also instills a sense of purpose and direction for the beneficiary.

A Collaborative Ecosystem

The initiative isn't just about collecting funds. It's about creating a supportive and structured ecosystem. Funds are managed in collaboration with support workers, ensuring that the monetary contributions are channeled productively, ultimately guiding individuals out of the cycle of homelessness.

Trust and Transparency

In philanthropy, trust is paramount. Donors are provided insights into where their contributions are utilized, fostering an environment of trust and reinforcing the belief that every penny is a step towards positive change.

A Beacon for the Future: Greater Change exemplifies the potential that arises when technology and compassion converge. It's not just about addressing the immediate needs but also about laying down a foundation for sustainable, long-term change.

In our collective quest to alleviate homelessness, Greater Change serves as a reminder. A reminder that innovation isn't just about technological advancements; it's about reimagining how we can better serve humanity. As we forge ahead, may such initiatives inspire us, challenge us, and spur us into action.

Ethical Considerations: Privacy, Data Ownership, and Digital Literacy

In an age of burgeoning technology and data-centric approaches, ethical considerations are paramount. As we integrate AI and other technological tools into the fight against homelessness, we must be acutely aware of the ethical landscape that surrounds their deployment. This section delves into three of the most pressing concerns: privacy, data ownership, and digital literacy.

Privacy

The push for data-driven solutions brings with it an increased demand for personal information. Data related to health, financial history, employment, and more can provide invaluable insights for predictive analyses. However, the acquisition and use of this data pose significant privacy concerns. Whose data is being collected? How is it being stored? Who has access to it? And for what purposes can it be used? Ensuring the privacy of individuals, particularly those already in vulnerable situations, is critical. This requires robust data encryption, strict access controls, and clear, informed consent mechanisms.

Data Ownership

In the digital age, data is often likened to a form of currency. It has value, both in its raw form and when processed. But who truly "owns" this data? Is it the individual it pertains to? The organization collecting it? Or the entity processing and analyzing it? These questions about data ownership are not just legal inquiries but ethical ones. It's crucial to establish transparent data ownership policies that prioritize the rights and interests of individuals, especially those at the forefront of the homelessness crisis.

Digital Literacy

As technology becomes increasingly interwoven into solutions for homelessness, there's a growing need to ensure that all stakeholders understand its implications. Digital literacy goes beyond just knowing how to use a device; it encompasses an understanding of the broader digital ecosystem, including the risks and benefits of data sharing, the workings of algorithms, and the potential biases inherent in technological solutions. Ensuring that both the providers of homelessness services and their beneficiaries have a degree of digital literacy is crucial. It empowers individuals to make informed decisions about their data and ensures that technological interventions are transparent and trusted.

While technology promises transformative solutions, it must always be deployed with a keen sense of ethical responsibility.

Tackling homelessness is a deeply human endeavor, and while we harness the power of data and AI, we must never lose sight of the individual rights, dignity, and aspirations of those we aim to assist. As we forge ahead, balancing technological prowess with ethical integrity will be the linchpin in creating compassionate, effective, and lasting solutions.

Chapter 3: Innovative Approaches to Ending Homelessness

The labyrinthine issue of homelessness, with its intricate tangle of causes and effects, demands an equally multifaceted approach to solutions. Throughout history, the challenge of ensuring every individual has a place to call home has stymied policymakers, community leaders, and activists. However, in our ever-evolving society, innovative strategies have emerged, turning traditional homeless intervention methods on their heads and offering hope for sustainable solutions.

In this chapter, we will delve into the paradigm-shifting "Housing-first" model. Is it truly the game-changer many claim it to be? How does it differ from past strategies, and what results has it achieved? We will also explore the profound impact of supportive housing and wraparound services, as these holistic approaches aim to address not just the symptom, but the root causes of homelessness.

Beyond theories and models, we'll journey across the world, diving into real-world case studies from various cities and countries. These narratives, rich with lessons and insights, provide tangible evidence of what works, what doesn't, and why. They serve as both a testament to human ingenuity and a call to action – reminding us that with the right strategies, the seemingly insurmountable challenge of homelessness can indeed be addressed.

Housing-first Models: A Game Changer?

In traditional approaches to homelessness, the common methodology was linear: individuals were expected to first address their personal issues, whether they were addiction, mental health, or unemployment, before they could be considered for long-term housing solutions. Essentially, housing was the reward for those who successfully navigated the system and achieved a certain level of "readiness." However, as well-intentioned as these systems may have been, they often overlooked a fundamental truth: stability is a precursor to recovery, not the other way around.

Enter the Housing-first model—a radical shift in philosophy that places housing as a primary intervention. At its core, Housing-first operates on the belief that everyone, regardless of their personal challenges or history, has a basic right to shelter. Instead of viewing housing as the end goal, this model sees it as the starting point. By providing individuals with a secure place to live without preconditions, the model creates an environment of stability, from which individuals can then begin to address other challenges they face, be it addiction, mental health, or employment barriers.

Early adopters of the Housing-first model reported significant success rates. Homeless individuals who were provided housing without preconditions had higher housing retention rates and showed notable improvements in mental health and overall well-being.

The economic benefits became evident as well. Studies revealed that the cost of providing housing, even without preconditions, was often lower than the societal costs incurred from emergency medical treatments, law enforcement, and other services frequently utilized by the homeless population.

While the accolades for the Housing-first approach are many, it's not without its critics. Some argue that without adequate support systems in place, simply placing someone in a home is not enough. Others voice concerns over potential misuse of resources or the model becoming a crutch rather than a steppingstone to self-sufficiency.

The conversation around Housing-first is undeniably shifting the landscape of homeless intervention. The model has forced societies globally to reevaluate deeply entrenched beliefs about homelessness, responsibility, and human rights. As we delve deeper, we will explore the nuances of this model, its implementation in various regions, its successes, and the challenges it still faces. Is Housing-first truly the game-changer in the fight against homelessness, or is it just one piece of a much larger puzzle?

Globally, countries and cities adopting this model are witnessing tangible changes. In places where Housing-first has been thoroughly implemented, emergency room visits have decreased, encounters with the criminal justice system have reduced, and individuals have reported enhanced life satisfaction and well-being. The economic argument too is strong. Savings made by decreasing the strain on medical, judicial, and other emergency services often outweigh the costs of providing housing directly.

The model's global adaptability presents another layer of complexity. Socio-cultural contexts, availability of resources, and differing definitions of homelessness mean the model cannot be a one-size-fits-all solution. For instance, the challenges and resources in urban U.S. cities might differ significantly from those in the rural parts of developing countries. This necessitates that while the core philosophy remains consistent, the practical applications and strategies might need significant tailoring.

The dialogue surrounding Housing-first brings forth pertinent questions about community integration, tenant rights, and the quality and location of housing. Is it enough to just provide a roof, or should the focus also encompass community-building, ensuring mental health services, and creating avenues for economic opportunities? Moreover, with housing as a primary right, how do we ensure that individuals are not isolated or pushed to the margins of society in poorly maintained or remotely located housings?

The efficacy of Housing-first, while promising, is still a topic of ongoing study and debate. It has certainly challenged the status quo, provoking global introspection on how societies view and address homelessness.

While its triumphs are celebrated, its challenges offer opportunities for refinement. The key lies in understanding that while Housing-first might be a monumental step in the right direction, the journey to eradicating homelessness requires a multifaceted, adaptable, and ever-evolving strategy.

The Power of Supportive Housing and Wraparound Services

Supportive housing is more than just a place to stay; it's a fusion of affordable housing and services meant to help people lead more stable, productive lives. The core belief behind supportive housing is that with the right foundation and assistance, those facing the most complex challenges can maintain stable housing. These challenges range from chronic homelessness, severe mental illnesses, multiple high-cost hospital stays, and repeated encounters with the criminal justice system. The "support" in supportive housing can manifest in various forms: mental health care, physical health care, job training, life skills, case management, or childcare.

Wraparound services are a crucial component of supportive housing, offering holistic and person-centered support. They're called "wraparound" because they quite literally wrap services around the individual, rather than forcing the individual to navigate a myriad of disjointed services on their own.

The philosophy is grounded in the belief that when services are tailored to the specific needs and wants of an individual or family, they are more effective, leading to improved outcomes and, often, cost savings.

This approach's success lies in its adaptability. The same family or individual might need varying supports at different times. A previously unemployed individual might first need job training and once employed, might require childcare or mental health services. The versatility of wraparound services ensures that as needs change, the support structure adapts accordingly.

The effectiveness of supportive housing isn't just about the sheer number or versatility of services. At its core, it's about building trust and relationships. For many, especially those who have experienced chronic homelessness, trust in systems and people might be eroded. The trauma-informed care commonly integrated into these services recognizes past traumas and seeks to rebuild trust, ensuring that individuals feel safe, respected, and in control.

As transformative as supportive housing can be it is not without challenges.

Funding and resource allocation remain persistent issues. The initial costs for these programs can be high, even though studies consistently show that they save communities money in the long run by reducing the strain on emergency services. Another challenge lies in coordination, ensuring that services truly are integrated and don't just operate in silos.

Supportive housing and wraparound services represent a holistic paradigm shift. They prompt societies to move beyond reactive measures, instead focusing on proactive, comprehensive interventions that truly get to the heart of the issues. The emphasis shifts from merely managing homelessness to creating environments where individuals can thrive and rebuild. It's an embodiment of the adage, "Give a man a fish, and you feed him for a day. Teach a man to fish, and you feed him for a lifetime."

Real-world Solutions: Case Studies from Different Cities and Countries

Case Study 1: The Helsinki Model for Eradicating Homelessness

In recent years, Helsinki, the capital city of Finland, has emerged as a beacon of hope in the global quest to address homelessness. The city's transformative approach hinges on the Housing First model, a stark departure from traditional strategies used in many other parts of the world. Instead of the conventional method, where individuals are transitioned through different stages of housing based on their readiness or perceived worthiness, Helsinki decided to provide a straightforward solution to homelessness: immediate housing.

In this paradigm shift, the idea is simple yet revolutionary. Rather than placing the city's homeless population in temporary shelters—a mere stop-gap solution—Helsinki authorities and social services opted to grant them permanent housing from the onset. The underlying belief of this initiative is rooted in the principle that having a stable, personal space is a fundamental human right, not a reward for good behavior or meeting certain criteria.

But the city didn't stop at just providing homes. Recognizing that homelessness often goes hand in hand with other complex issues, including mental health challenges, substance abuse, and socio-economic struggles, Helsinki complemented its housing initiative with tailored support services. These services ranged from counseling and healthcare to vocational training, ensuring that individuals weren't merely housed but were also supported in their journey towards stability and personal fulfillment.

The outcome of this bold and compassionate approach has been nothing short of remarkable. Helsinki has witnessed a significant reduction in homelessness, positioning itself as a global exemplar. This success story underscores the transformative power of policies that prioritize human dignity, challenging traditional notions of homelessness intervention and inspiring cities worldwide to reimagine their strategies.

Case Study 2: Utah's Triumph Over Chronic Homelessness

Utah, one of the United States' geographically expansive states, has made international headlines not for its scenic beauty, but for its groundbreaking approach to tackling chronic homelessness. While many U.S. states grappled with rising homeless numbers, Utah took a leap of faith in the early 2000s by embracing the Housing First model—a decision that led to profound, positive change.

At the heart of Utah's decision was a surprising revelation. State analyses uncovered that the financial strain of chronic homelessness on public resources was far more than previously assumed. The transient nature of homelessness meant that many individuals without stable housing frequently relied on costly public services. These included emergency room visits, with the inevitable health complications that life on the streets can bring, and the criminal justice system, as minor infractions led to repeated jail time. When the numbers were crunched, it became evident that the indirect costs of leaving people on the streets vastly surpassed the costs of providing them with permanent housing.

Emboldened by this data, Utah launched a version of the Housing First model. Instead of mandating sobriety or employment as prerequisites for housing—a common stipulation in many other regions—the state offered unconditional housing. The rationale was direct: to address the myriad challenges associated with homelessness, a stable living environment was essential.

Coupled with this housing initiative were critical support services tailored to the varied needs of the newly housed residents. From addiction counseling to job training programs, these services sought to holistically address the root causes of homelessness and ensure long-term stability.

By 2015, the results were astonishing. Utah proudly reported a nearly 91% decrease in chronic homelessness—a testament to the state's innovative and compassionate approach. Utah's experience serves as a compelling reminder that sometimes, the most direct solution is the most effective. In prioritizing the well-being of its most vulnerable residents, Utah not only transformed countless lives but also showcased the economic logic and humanitarian promise of the Housing First model.

Case Study 3: Melbourne's "Journey to Social Inclusion" - A Holistic Approach to Long-term Homelessness

Melbourne, a cosmopolitan hub known for its art, culture, and coffee, has also grappled with the universal challenge of homelessness. Among its varied responses stands the "Journey to Social Inclusion" (J2SI) program, an initiative that has not just addressed the surface issues of homelessness but has delved deep into its roots.

Conceived by the Sacred Heart Mission, a stalwart in Melbourne's social services landscape, J2SI was a response to the realization that traditional short-term interventions, while essential, were not enough to break the cycle of long-term homelessness. The individuals who found themselves on the streets for extended periods often had complex, intertwined challenges—mental health issues, addiction, trauma, and a history of unstable employment. It was clear that a more intensive, holistic solution was required.

J2SI's approach was groundbreaking in its comprehensiveness. Instead of offering piecemeal services, participants were enveloped in a wraparound care model. First and foremost, they received help in finding stable, long-term housing—a foundation upon which other interventions could be effectively built.

With the stability of a home secured, participants were then connected with a range of vital services tailored to their unique needs. Mental health services addressed trauma and ongoing psychological challenges. Addiction treatment provided pathways out of substance dependency. Vocational training and employment assistance programs offered a bridge to economic stability and social reintegration.

The results spoke for themselves. Not only did a significant majority of J2SI participants remain housed, but they also reported marked improvements in their overall health, mental well-being, and sense of community connection. Moreover, many found purpose in employment, further integrating them into the fabric of Melbourne's diverse society.

Melbourne's J2SI program showcases the transformative power of holistic interventions. By addressing the multi-dimensional challenges faced by those entrenched in long-term homelessness, the Sacred Heart Mission demonstrated that with the right support, everyone has the potential to rebuild and thrive.

Case Study 4: Calgary's Ambitious Decade-Long Quest to End Homelessness

In the heart of Alberta lies Calgary, a city celebrated for its bustling energy sector, the iconic Calgary Stampede, and a community-driven spirit that never shies away from challenges. This resilience was on full display when, in 2008, Calgary boldly launched its "10-Year Plan to End Homelessness".

Rather than opting for a piecemeal approach, Calgary's visionaries recognized that eradicating homelessness required a multifaceted strategy, where each piece, in tandem, could create a tapestry of change. At the heart of this initiative was the philosophy that every citizen deserves the dignity of a roof over their head.

Key to the plan was the adoption of the rapid rehousing approach, a model that prioritized swiftly moving individuals from streets and shelters into stable, permanent housing. But the city was astute in realizing that merely providing housing was a starting point, not a conclusion. The real challenge lay in ensuring that once individuals were rehoused, they remained housed. As such, Calgary made significant investments in follow-up support services tailored to the diverse needs of its homeless population.

The gamut of these services was extensive: mental health interventions, addiction treatments, job training, and community integration programs, to name a few. By addressing the root causes that often precipitate homelessness, Calgary aimed to break the cyclical nature of the problem.

The outcomes of this 10-year journey have been commendable. Not only did Calgary witness a tangible reduction in its homeless numbers, but the initiative also served as a beacon, shining light on the city's commitment to its citizens and providing a blueprint for other municipalities looking to tackle similar challenges.

Today, Calgary stands as a testament to the idea that with a combination of vision, planning, community involvement, and persistence, cities can make significant strides in their battle against homelessness.

Case Study 5: Tokyo's New Start - Reintegrating the Homeless Through Work and Support

Tokyo, the bustling capital of Japan, represents an interplay of tradition and modernity. Yet, even in this city of wonders, the shadows of homelessness have persisted. As the metropolis surged forward, its underbelly revealed a growing number of citizens disconnected from its prosperity. Recognizing this burgeoning crisis, a pivotal initiative was launched: The New Start Program.

The New Start Program emerged not just as another non-profit but as a beacon of hope for Tokyo's homeless. Central to its ethos was the belief that homelessness wasn't just about lacking a roof; it was about being detached from society's rhythm. To reintegrate its beneficiaries, New Start decided to address homelessness from multiple angles: housing, employment, and psychological support.

At the forefront of the program is its unique employment model. Understanding the debilitating effect of joblessness on an individual's psyche, New Start doesn't just offer job training; it actively integrates the homeless into its business ventures. From roles in recycling operations to roles in logistics and retail, beneficiaries are provided opportunities to be active contributors to the very fabric of Tokyo's economic life.

New Start's brilliance lies in its comprehensive approach. Beyond employment, participants are offered stable housing, ensuring they have a secure environment to rebuild their lives. Simultaneously, counseling sessions offer emotional and psychological support, aiding individuals in navigating the often-complex journey from homelessness to stability.

This integrative strategy has seen numerous success stories, with many beneficiaries not only finding stable employment but also rekindling connections with their families and society at large.

Tokyo's New Start Program epitomizes the notion that addressing homelessness requires more than just immediate relief. It's about restoring dignity, purpose, and a sense of belonging. Through its holistic approach, New Start continues to reshape lives, reiterating that with the right support, every individual can find their way back into society's embrace.

Case Study 6: Vienna's Visionary Approach to Housing - Social Equity through Affordable Living

In the heart of Europe, Vienna stands not just as a symbol of art, culture, and history, but also as a beacon of progressive urban planning. Among the city's most laudable initiatives is its transformative Social Housing Program. At a time when urban spaces globally grapple with soaring housing prices and increasing homelessness, Vienna offers a model of sustainable living anchored in social justice.

Vienna's journey in reshaping its urban landscape began nearly a century ago, post-World War I, but its most remarkable achievement lies in its sustained commitment to housing as a fundamental right. Today, the city is a testament to this commitment, with approximately 60% of its residents living in homes that are municipally built, owned, or managed.

What sets Vienna's Social Housing Program apart isn't just the vast scale of its reach; it's the underlying philosophy. Homes aren't just built; they are woven into the fabric of the city's architectural and cultural heritage. These aren't mere housing blocks; they are well-designed spaces with access to green areas, community centers, and amenities. They cater not just to the city's economically challenged but are open to a wide cross-section of society, fostering a sense of community and reducing social segregation.

Rent structures in these homes further underscore Vienna's commitment to social equity. They are meticulously calibrated based on income, ensuring that housing remains affordable irrespective of economic status. This means that a vast segment of the population, from artists to teachers, from students to senior citizens, finds a place in Vienna's social housing spectrum.

The success of Vienna's Social Housing Program can be gauged not just by its longevity and scale but by its impact on the city's social fabric. In Vienna, affordable housing isn't a mere policy; it's a way of life. By ensuring that a majority of its residents live in homes they can afford, Vienna has cultivated a sense of belonging, community, and stability.

As urban centers around the world grapple with housing crises, Vienna's Social Housing Program stands as a testament to the power of visionary planning, sustained commitment, and the belief that housing, beyond being a basic need, is a cornerstone of social cohesion and harmony.

Highlights from Case Studies from Different Cities and Countries

Helsinki, Finland

Helsinki has almost eradicated homelessness using the Housing First model. Instead of placing homeless people in temporary shelters, the city provided them with permanent housing right away. Additionally, they were provided with tailored support services. The results were impressive, with a significant reduction in homelessness.

Utah, USA
Utah also implemented a version of the Housing First model. The state found that providing homeless people with permanent housing was cheaper than the cumulative costs of emergency room visits, jail time, and other services the homeless population typically requires. By 2015, the state reported a nearly 91% decrease in chronic homelessness.

Melbourne, Australia
"Journey to Social Inclusion" program. This initiative by the Sacred Heart Mission provided intensive, tailored support to people who had been homeless for long periods. Participants received help finding housing and were given access to mental health services, addiction treatment, and assistance finding employment. The program reported positive outcomes, with many participants staying housed and seeing improvements in their health and well-being.

Calgary, Canada
Calgary's 10-Year Plan to End Homelessness. Launched in 2008, the city's plan incorporated various strategies, including prevention, rehousing, and support services. The emphasis was on a rapid rehousing approach, moving people quickly from the streets or shelters into permanent housing, then providing the necessary support. The initiative has seen a reduction in homelessness in Calgary.

Tokyo, Japan

Created the New Start Program. This non-profit offers employment, housing, and counseling to people who have lost their homes. The initiative focuses on integrating the homeless back into society by providing job training and opportunities to work in New Start's businesses.

Vienna, Austria
Created a Social Housing Program. Vienna has been celebrated for its social housing program, where around 60% of the population lives in municipally built, owned, or managed homes. Rent is based on income, ensuring housing affordability for a vast segment of the population.

The global approach to addressing homelessness and housing instability is as diverse as the cities themselves. Each metropolis, with its unique socio-cultural fabric, resources, and challenges, has tailored solutions to resonate with its population, always striving for a society where everyone has a place to call home.

Helsinki's resounding success echoes the power of directly confronting homelessness through the Housing First model, where the provision of permanent housing was augmented by dedicated support services. Such a comprehensive approach highlights that ending homelessness isn't solely about brick-and-mortar structures, but the holistic rehabilitation of individuals, addressing not just their housing needs but also their mental, emotional, and economic well-being.

On the other side of the globe, Utah, USA, bolstered by hard data, shifted paradigms by highlighting the economic rationality of Housing First. By demonstrating that providing housing could be more cost-effective than bearing the cascading costs of homelessness, Utah presented a compelling argument that combined compassion with economic sense.

Melbourne's "Journey to Social Inclusion" program reminds us that extended homelessness often weaves complex webs of challenges. Addressing these intricacies requires not just a roof overhead but also multifaceted support ranging from mental health to employment assistance.

Similarly, Calgary's rapid rehousing focus in their 10-Year Plan showcased the importance of swift interventions, reducing the duration individuals or families spend homeless or in temporary shelters. The faster the rehousing, the quicker the healing and reintegration process can begin.

Tokyo and Vienna, while different in their approaches, both emphasized the vital role of societal integration. Tokyo's New Start Program tackled homelessness by focusing on reintegrating individuals into the workforce and society, thus providing them not just with shelter but with purpose and dignity. Vienna, in its century-long commitment to housing, created a vibrant mosaic of inclusivity, ensuring housing affordability across its socio-economic spectrum, demonstrating that urban development and social equity can, indeed, go hand in hand.

Drawing insights from these cities paints a picture of hope. Whether through policy reimagining, societal interventions, or technology, the challenge of homelessness is being met with innovation, empathy, and determination. These case studies serve as beacons, guiding other cities and regions, showing that with concerted efforts, strategic planning, and, most importantly, the will to act, homelessness can be a challenge of the past. The road ahead, as these cities show, is one of collaborative action, sustained commitment, and a belief in the basic human right to a home.

Chapter 4: Collaborative Partnerships and Community Engagement

In the multifaceted landscape of homelessness intervention, no single entity possesses all the resources, perspectives, or expertise required to wholly address the issue. The journey towards eradicating homelessness is not one to be undertaken in isolation but requires a coming together of various stakeholders—be they governmental bodies, private enterprises, non-profit organizations, or the homeless individuals themselves. This chapter underscores the power and promise of collaborative partnerships and the transformative potential of community engagement in this domain.

Delving into successful collaborations, we will be enlightened by stories that highlight the tangible impacts of concerted efforts, underscoring the immense potential of pooling resources and wisdom. Furthermore, the importance of incorporating the voices of the homeless population in decision-making processes cannot be overemphasized. Their lived experiences provide invaluable insights that can lead to more effective and empathetic solutions. And as the boundaries between public and private sectors blur, we also explore the evolving landscape of public-private partnerships. Are they the blueprint for future successes in addressing homelessness?

Successful Collaborations: Stories of Impact

When diverse stakeholders converge with a shared goal, the results can be transformative. Successful collaborations in the realm of homelessness intervention have underscored this, demonstrating the efficacy of collective action. These stories, from different corners of the globe, tell tales not just of financial resources combined, but of expertise shared, best practices exchanged, and challenges addressed through creative problem-solving.

San Francisco, a city renowned for its tech innovations and affluence, has also grappled with a notable homelessness crisis. In response to this challenge, an innovative synergy emerged between diverse stakeholders: local businesses, NGOs, and the municipal government. Recognizing that traditional shelter models, with their restrictive timings and limited services, often failed to address the holistic needs of the homeless population, these entities collaborated to launch the 'Navigation Centers'.

These Navigation Centers are a departure from conventional shelters in multiple ways. Open 24/7, they cater to the inherent unpredictability of life on the streets. Homeless individuals don't just find a place to sleep; they find a place where they can feel secure at any hour, breaking the cycle of nightly searches for safe refuge.

But it's not just the round-the-clock accessibility that sets Navigation Centers apart. They are meticulously designed to be hubs of comprehensive services. Medical professionals are available onsite, ensuring that health issues, often exacerbated by life on the streets, are promptly addressed. Legal counselors assist with matters like identification documentation, housing rights, and in some cases, immigration issues. Mental health professionals and substance abuse counselors provide vital support, recognizing that many homeless individuals grapple with psychological challenges or addictions.

Moreover, these centers emphasize dignity and agency. Spaces are designed to be more private and accommodating, recognizing that many homeless individuals have experienced trauma and need environments where they feel safe and respected. By allowing partners, pets, and possessions, which many shelters prohibit, they address some of the primary barriers that deter homeless individuals from seeking shelter.

The result of this holistic approach is evident in its outcomes. Navigation Centers have not only provided immediate relief but have also served as effective conduits to more permanent housing solutions. By establishing trust and addressing a broad spectrum of needs, they have successfully enabled many homeless individuals to transition to stable living situations more rapidly than traditional shelters ever did. The San Francisco model underscores the profound impact of not just providing shelter, but offering a comprehensive, empathetic support system.

In **Birmingham,** a city deeply embedded with cultural and community-oriented values, the stark realities of homelessness became particularly pronounced during the frigid winter months. As temperatures plummeted, the vulnerabilities of the city's homeless population became dangerously magnified. Recognizing the dire need for a solution, a unique collaboration emerged, bringing together diverse entities: faith groups of various denominations, spirited community volunteers, and the proactive Birmingham City Council.

This alliance led to the conception and execution of the Winter Shelter Program. Instead of being anchored to one location, this initiative adopted a rotating model. Different churches, temples, mosques, and community centers opened their doors in succession, transforming their spaces into warm, welcoming shelters for the homeless. The idea was innovative in its simplicity. It tapped into Birmingham's robust network of faith and community organizations, allowing resources to be spread out and ensuring no single institution bore the brunt of the responsibility.

But the Winter Shelter Program wasn't just about offering a reprieve from the cold. It was about warmth in a more profound sense. Guests, as they were often referred to, were treated with dignity and respect. Spaces were prepared with care, ensuring comfort and cleanliness. Volunteers and faith leaders would often engage in heart-to-heart conversations, providing emotional support and a listening ear.

Beyond the immediate sheltering, the program integrated services that looked towards a more sustainable solution for its beneficiaries. Counseling services were made available, addressing both the psychological trauma many homeless individuals carried and the practical challenges they faced. There was a recognition that homelessness wasn't just a consequence of economic challenges, but often interwoven with mental health issues, personal tragedies, and systemic failures.

One of the standout features of the program was its emphasis on reintegration. Job placement workshops were organized, and connections were made with local employers willing to give a chance to those trying to rebuild their lives. Skill training sessions were also facilitated, aimed at equipping individuals with practical abilities that could pave the way for steady employment.

The success of Birmingham's Winter Shelter Program lay in its multi-faceted approach. It didn't just see homelessness as a singular problem but understood it as a complex issue demanding a multi-pronged response. By bringing together the strengths of faith groups, the dynamism of community volunteers, and the organizational prowess of the city council, Birmingham demonstrated how collaborative endeavors can lead to impactful, compassionate solutions.

Bogotá, Colombia's sprawling capital, has long been emblematic of a city in flux. From its high-altitude views to its bustling streets, Bogotá pulses with a blend of historical richness and modern aspirations. However, like many urban centers worldwide, the city grappled with areas that had fallen into neglect, spaces that became associated more with criminal activities and vagrancy than community interaction.

It was in these very pockets of neglect that an innovative vision started taking shape. A confluence of minds - progressive urban planners, passionate homeless advocates, and skilled local artisans - saw potential where many only saw problems. They envisioned these disused public spaces not as dead ends, but as untapped canvases awaiting transformation.

Initiating the project, urban planners first assessed the spatial and logistical aspects of these zones. They identified spaces that could be redesigned to accommodate communal activities while being environmentally sustainable and accessible. At the same time, homeless advocates ensured that the project would be inclusive, bringing those who had been marginalized right to the center of the rejuvenation efforts.

Local artisans, the bearers of Bogotá's rich cultural tapestry, became the bridge between the past and the present. They brought in their crafts, painting murals that told stories of the city's history, its indigenous roots, its colonial past, and its hopes for the future. These murals, alongside installations made from recycled materials, gave each space a distinctive identity.

But perhaps the most heartwarming aspect of the entire endeavor was the involvement of formerly homeless individuals. They weren't just passive beneficiaries; they became active contributors. Many were trained in basic construction and landscaping, playing a role in the physical transformation of the spaces. Others, with a penchant for the arts, collaborated with artisans in crafting installations or even performing at community events.

These rejuvenated areas became more than just visually appealing spaces. They evolved into thriving community hubs where art exhibitions, cultural workshops, and social events were regularly held. Children could be seen attending art classes, while adults participated in community discussions or simply enjoyed the serene environment.

The ex-homeless individuals, once seen as mere occupants of these spaces, became their custodians. They took charge of maintaining the gardens, overseeing event setups, and even conducting guided tours, explaining the historical and cultural significance of the various installations. Their involvement underscored a sense of ownership and pride, not just for themselves but for the broader community that had once shunned them.

Bogotá's transformation of these public spaces didn't just bring about a physical change; it facilitated a societal shift. It rewove the fabric of the community, making it more inclusive and vibrant. The initiative highlighted how, with vision and collaboration, cities can turn challenges into opportunities, creating spaces that resonate with history, culture, and a shared sense of belonging.

Such stories illuminate the spectrum of possibilities when collaboration is prioritized. They remind us that addressing homelessness requires more than resources; it demands vision, creativity, and the commitment to working hand-in-hand. As varied as these collaborative approaches are, they share a common thread: the belief in collective power and the understanding that together, communities can craft solutions that are both impactful and sustainable.

Engaging the Homeless Population in Decision-making

In addressing the intricacies of homelessness, the inclusion of the very individuals facing this plight in decision-making processes is not just an ethical imperative but also a practical one.

Tackling homelessness from an external standpoint without involving the lived experiences of those affected can lead to misaligned solutions, fostering inefficacies and potential misallocations of resources.

When cities and organizations take the step to actively involve the homeless population in shaping the solutions, they tap into a wellspring of insight that can radically reshape interventions.

Take the case of **Portland, Oregon**. Known for its progressive approach to various societal issues, the city-initiated dialogue sessions where homeless individuals were invited to share their experiences and suggest areas of improvement. These weren't just tokenistic gatherings; they were structured, facilitated meetings where every voice was given equal weight. What emerged was a clearer understanding of the gaps in the current system – from the restrictive hours of operation of some shelters that didn't cater to those working odd hours, to the need for more pet-friendly accommodations, as many homeless individuals relied on their pets for emotional support.

In **Manchester, UK**, a program was introduced where homeless individuals were trained as researchers. Armed with clipboards, cameras, and interview guides, they took to the streets, not just to share their stories, but to collect the narratives of others like them. This peer-led research approach led to a trove of qualitative data, shedding light on the nuances of homelessness in the city – from the locations deemed safest for sleeping to the bureaucratic hurdles faced when trying to access public services. The findings from this initiative were then presented to the city council and played a pivotal role in shaping Manchester's subsequent homelessness strategies.

Beyond these structured initiatives, some cities have also created platforms for continuous feedback. Digital kiosks in places like San Diego and mobile apps in regions of Scandinavia allow homeless individuals to rate shelters, drop-in centers, and other facilities. This real-time feedback mechanism ensures that service providers can be more agile in their response, making necessary changes swiftly.

However, the process of engaging the homeless population in decision-making isn't without its challenges. Building trust is paramount, as many homeless individuals may have faced years of stigmatization, marginalization, and, at times, outright hostility from authorities and the public. They need to be assured that their voices will genuinely be heard and that their involvement will lead to tangible outcomes. It's also essential to ensure representation, ensuring that the diverse subgroups within the homeless community – be it veterans, LGBTQ+ individuals, or ethnic minorities – are given an equal platform.

When cities and organizations prioritize the active participation of the homeless in decision-making processes, they're not just empowering this marginalized group; they're fortifying their strategies with ground-level insights.

It's a symbiotic relationship where both parties stand to benefit – the homeless population feels seen, heard, and valued, while policymakers and service providers gain a deeper, more nuanced understanding of the issue they're trying to address.

Public-Private Partnerships: A Blueprint for Success?

Public-Private Partnerships (PPPs) have increasingly become an instrumental tool in addressing societal issues, combining the strengths and resources of both the public and private sectors. In the realm of homelessness, these partnerships can pave the way for innovative solutions, bridge funding gaps, and foster more holistic approaches. However, while the potential of PPPs is vast, so too are the complexities involved. It's essential to examine both their advantages and the challenges they present.

The allure of PPPs in addressing homelessness is multi-fold. For one, the private sector, with its efficiencies, technological prowess, and capital, can provide the infrastructure and tools that public agencies might lack. Tech companies can offer data analytics and AI capabilities to better understand homeless populations and predict trends. Real estate developers can assist in creating affordable housing units or repurposing existing structures. Financial institutions might offer low-interest loans or funding mechanisms that make housing projects feasible.

One example is in **Los Angeles,** where rising homelessness rates compelled the city to seek unconventional solutions. A partnership was struck with a consortium of developers, financiers, and non-profits to expedite the construction of affordable housing units. Leveraging private capital, the project aimed to cut the typical development timeline in half, ensuring rapid response to the burgeoning crisis.

However, beyond mere resources, PPPs also bring a diversity of perspectives to the table. With stakeholders from various backgrounds collaborating, solutions tend to be more multifaceted, addressing not just the symptoms but the root causes of homelessness.

In **Seattle**, a tech giant partnered with local NGOs to establish a homeless shelter within its corporate campus. But it wasn't just about providing a roof over heads; the company also leveraged its technological expertise to set up job training programs, aiming to reintegrate homeless individuals into the workforce. Such integrative approaches, looking beyond immediate relief to long-term solutions, typify the best of what PPPs can offer.

The path isn't devoid of pitfalls. Public and private entities often operate with different mandates, timelines, and expectations. While public agencies are beholden to citizens and tend to have longer bureaucratic processes, private companies are accountable to shareholders and might seek quicker returns on investment. This divergence can lead to tensions, with disagreements on project priorities, timelines, and outcomes.

There's a vital need to ensure transparency and accountability in these partnerships. The involvement of private entities, particularly profit-driven ones, in a deeply societal issue like homelessness can arouse skepticism. Concerns about potential profiteering, or the private sector wielding undue influence over public policy, are valid. Thus, clear governance structures, open communication, and defined roles become paramount.

Public-Private Partnerships, when navigated with care, hold the promise of transformative change in the battle against homelessness. They embody the adage that the whole is greater than the sum of its parts. Yet, the onus is on both public and private stakeholders to approach these collaborations with transparency, mutual respect, and a shared vision. Only then can PPPs truly serve as a blueprint for success in this noble endeavor.

Chapter 5: Policy and Legal Frameworks for Homelessness Eradication

The pursuit of a just and equitable society places on its leaders and citizens the duty to address systemic challenges, and homelessness stands prominently among these. At the heart of resolving this issue lies a complex web of policies and legal frameworks that either contribute to alleviating the problem or inadvertently exacerbate it. Addressing homelessness is not just about providing shelter; it's about understanding and rectifying the intricate and often systemic factors that lead to such dire circumstances in the first place.

In this chapter, we embark on a comprehensive exploration of the existing policy landscape that surrounds homelessness. We will delve into the intricate maze of legal structures, examining how they have evolved over time, their successes, and the unintended challenges they might have introduced. With each policy, a reflection of society's priorities and values emerges, and through this reflection, we can gain insight into the dynamics between societal intent, policy implementation, and real-world outcomes.

Beyond merely understanding policies, this chapter aims to shine a light on the lives that are affected by them. With homelessness so deeply intertwined with issues of mental health, substance abuse, and poverty, it becomes imperative to understand the intersectionality of these challenges. How do policies cater to those grappling with mental health issues or substance abuse? Is the specter of poverty addressed merely as an economic challenge, or are its profound social implications recognized and addressed?

While retrospection is vital, anticipation and foresight are equally critical. As we look to the future, what are the emergent challenges that policies need to address? What gaps exist in current legal frameworks that might become chasms of inequality in the future? How can we, as a society, better predict and preempt the challenges of tomorrow?

As we navigate through this chapter, we will be presented with not just a series of facts and observations but a call to action. A call to reimagine, redesign, and reconstruct the policy frameworks that can steer us closer to a world where homelessness is a relic of the past. Through this exploration, we hope to foster a deeper understanding of the delicate interplay between policymaking, societal values, and the lives of those most vulnerable among us.

An Overview of World Existing Policies and Their Outcomes

As nations grapple with the persistent issue of homelessness, a myriad of policy approaches has emerged across the globe. These strategies, while rooted in unique socio-economic, cultural, and political contexts, share a common objective: the eradication of homelessness. By examining these policies, their successes, failures, and the lessons they offer, we can gain invaluable insights into the global effort to combat this pressing concern.

North America: Both the U.S. and Canada have largely oscillated between remedial and preventative approaches. The U.S. has seen a shift from policies primarily focused on emergency response, like shelters, to more holistic, long-term strategies such as the 'Housing First' model. The results, while promising in areas like Utah, have been inconsistent nationwide. Canada, with its National Housing Strategy, has pledged billions to cut chronic homelessness in half, showing significant commitment at the federal level.

Europe: Many European nations have embraced a human-rights-based approach to homelessness. Finland's Housing First policy, as previously discussed, has been a trailblazer, demonstrating that investing in long-term housing solutions can drastically reduce homelessness. Conversely, countries like Hungary have faced criticism for policies that penalize the homeless rather than assisting them, illustrating the vast policy disparities even within a seemingly cohesive continent.

Asia: The Asian continent offers a diverse range of policy responses. While Japan's welfare-oriented approach focuses on providing employment opportunities and social integration, other nations, grappling with rapid urbanization, are still in the early stages of policy formulation. The efforts in regions like South Korea, emphasizing rehabilitation and community support, highlight the importance of culturally tailored solutions.

Australia and New Zealand: These nations, while geographically close, have markedly different policy landscapes. Australia's focus on "rough sleepers" has been complemented by initiatives targeting the hidden homeless, such as those in temporary accommodations. New Zealand, confronting a rising housing crisis, has been experimenting with innovative solutions, from pop-up houses to large-scale investment in affordable housing projects.

Africa: African nations, facing a plethora of developmental challenges, have a complex relationship with homelessness. South Africa, post-apartheid, has made strides with progressive housing policies, though implementation remains a challenge. Other countries, amidst economic and political turmoil, see homelessness as part of larger issues, like internal displacement due to conflict.

South America: Rapid urbanization, combined with socio-economic disparities, has led to significant homelessness in many South American cities. Brazil's approach, integrating the homeless in city development projects, contrasts with more punitive policies in other regions.

In reflecting upon these diverse policies, a few key insights emerge. Firstly, one-size-fits-all solutions are elusive. The success of a policy often hinges on its adaptability to local contexts. Secondly, while reactive measures provide immediate relief, proactive and preventive policies tend to yield more sustainable outcomes. Lastly, the involvement of the homeless population in policymaking, ensuring their perspectives and needs are central, is often a hallmark of the most effective strategies. In the subsequent sections, we will delve deeper into the intricacies of these policies, revealing the complexities inherent in transforming intent into impactful action.

Europe's Diverse Response to Homelessness

Europe, with its rich tapestry of cultures, histories, and socio-political landscapes, presents a fascinating study in contrasts when it comes to addressing homelessness. The continent's approach, while largely rooted in the principles of human rights and social welfare, varies considerably from one nation to another.

The Nordic Model: At one end of the spectrum lies the Nordic model, exemplified by Finland's pioneering Housing First policy. This approach, founded on the principle that every individual has an inherent right to housing, posits that stable housing is the first step in addressing other challenges, be they financial, health-related, or social. By offering unconditional housing, without requiring recipients to first address substance abuse or other issues, Finland has seen a remarkable reduction in homelessness. This success is attributed not just to the policy itself, but also to the robust social welfare system that supports it, ensuring that individuals have access to health care, education, and employment opportunities.

The Central European Challenge: Venturing into Central Europe, the picture becomes more complex. Hungary, for instance, has taken measures that are seen by many as regressive. The country's controversial decision to criminalize street homelessness has drawn sharp criticism from human rights organizations globally. Instead of providing support and resources to aid the homeless population, such policies push them further into the margins, exacerbating their vulnerabilities and making reintegration into society even more challenging.

Western Europe's Mixed Bag: Western European nations like France, Germany, and the UK have adopted multifaceted approaches. While there are comprehensive welfare systems in place, urban centers in these countries still grapple with visible homelessness. These nations have invested in emergency shelters, temporary housing, and rehabilitation programs. However, the challenge remains substantial, especially with factors like migration, high living costs in cities, and limited affordable housing.

The Southern Perspective: In Southern Europe, countries like Greece, Italy, and Spain, already strained by economic challenges, have seen a rise in homelessness following the financial crisis of the late 2000s. With state resources stretched thin, community organizations, religious groups, and NGOs have stepped in to fill the void, offering shelters, food programs, and vocational training.

In synthesizing Europe's multifaceted response to homelessness, it becomes evident that while the continent as a whole acknowledges the gravity of the issue, strategies to address it are profoundly influenced by regional histories, economic capacities, societal values, and political will. The European narrative underscores the importance of context-specific solutions, robust social safety nets, and a commitment to upholding the dignity and rights of every individual.

The Complex Tapestry of Homelessness and Policy Responses

Understanding homelessness requires peeling back layers of interrelated challenges. It's an issue deeply intertwined with mental health, substance abuse, and poverty – three domains that are themselves heavily influenced by policy decisions. Each of these aspects doesn't operate in a vacuum; they frequently compound one another, creating a maze of obstacles for those trapped within.

Homelessness at its core represents a failure of systems, an intersection of structural, personal, and economic challenges that culminate in a profound crisis for the individuals ensnared within its confines. This predicament is further complicated by the matrix of mental health issues, substance abuse, and poverty – formidable adversaries that magnify the intricacies of the problem.

Each strand in this complex tapestry of homelessness is woven together, feeding into and off of each other. For instance, the mental health struggles of an individual might render them more susceptible to substance abuse, which, in turn, could exacerbate their economic vulnerabilities, pushing them into the precipice of homelessness. Simultaneously, societal structures, shaped by policies and historical determinants, can either offer a safety net or present insurmountable barriers.

The mosaic of homelessness isn't static; it evolves over time, influenced by shifting economic tides, changing policy landscapes, and societal perceptions. The rise of gig economies, erosion of social welfare systems, or changes in housing policies can either fortify or fray this intricate web.

As we delve deeper into the exploration of homelessness and its policy responses, it becomes imperative to approach it with a multifaceted lens. We must recognize and dissect the interconnectedness of its various components, acknowledging that a solution in one domain might inadvertently trigger challenges in another. It is only by understanding this intricate interplay, by tracing the threads that bind the tapestry, can we begin to envision and engineer holistic, sustainable solutions that address the root causes and not just the symptoms of homelessness.

The Mental Health Link

Historically, the nexus between homelessness and mental health has been a sore point in policymaking. In many countries during the mid-20th century, deinstitutionalization meant that a significant number of individuals with severe mental health disorders were released from state-run psychiatric facilities. The idea was to shift towards community-based care. However, due to inadequate preparation and resource allocation, many ended up on the streets, without the necessary support structures in place.

Modern policies have been trying to bridge this gap, but challenges remain. Ensuring that those with mental health conditions have access to appropriate care, housing, and social services is a complex endeavor. Furthermore, the stigma attached to mental illness can make it challenging for sufferers to seek help, maintain employment, or sustain relationships, often pushing them closer to homelessness.

The ramifications of these historical missteps are still felt today. While the intention behind deinstitutionalization was to reintegrate individuals into society and move away from isolating them, the lack of foresight and accompanying resources transformed what could have been a positive shift into a crisis. City streets became the unintended asylums for many, with public spaces turning into makeshift shelters for those grappling with severe psychological conditions.

Lessons have been learned. In recent decades, various countries and cities have made concerted efforts to revisit this nexus and design policies that are both compassionate and effective.

Mobile mental health units, for example, have been launched in certain areas to reach out to those on the streets, offering immediate counseling and guidance.

Similarly, 'Housing First' models, such as those implemented in Finland, combine housing with mental health support, underscoring the understanding that stability is foundational to recovery.

Community-based care, the original goal of deinstitutionalization, is seeing a resurgence but with a more informed approach.

Grassroots organizations and NGOs are partnering with local governments to create community centers that not only offer therapy and psychiatric care but also vocational training, helping individuals regain their independence. These centers operate on inclusivity, ensuring everyone, regardless of their mental health status, is treated with dignity and respect.

Stigma remains a formidable adversary. Media portrayal, societal prejudices, and a lack of widespread understanding about mental health conditions have fortified barriers.

Advocacy and awareness campaigns, helmed by both governmental bodies and civil society, are crucial. Schools, workplaces, and community institutions need to play active roles in debunking myths about mental illness and in fostering environments of acceptance.

Looking ahead, the vision is clear: to create societies where mental health is neither a taboo nor a ticket to homelessness.

This vision demands concerted collaboration, informed policymaking, and, most importantly, an unwavering commitment to viewing each individual beyond their conditions – as humans deserving of care, understanding, and a place to call home.

The Substance Abuse Dilemma

Substance abuse and its interplay with homelessness is a multifaceted issue that demands a nuanced understanding. The streets are often a refuge for those escaping traumatic or untenable situations, and in the midst of the despair and isolation that comes with homelessness, substances can offer a fleeting escape from reality. For some, it may start as an occasional relief but can quickly spiral into a full-blown addiction, further entrenching their state of destitution.

Those already grappling with addiction can find maintaining stable housing increasingly challenging. The financial strain of supporting a drug habit, combined with the societal stigma and ostracization associated with addiction, can sever ties with family and friends, often leading individuals to lose their foundational support systems. As a result, they become increasingly vulnerable, with their primary focus on obtaining the next high rather than seeking shelter or employment.

Historically, the prevailing approach to addressing substance abuse was punitive. Policies focused on penalizing users, leading to a cycle of arrests, brief incarcerations, and subsequent releases back onto the streets, with no real intervention or support. Such policies, rather than curbing the issue, magnified it, pushing users further to society's fringes, making outreach and rehabilitation even more challenging.

The global perspective on addiction is slowly shifting. More jurisdictions are beginning to recognize it as a public health issue rather than a mere criminal act. Cities like Vancouver, Canada, with its Insite program, have pioneered the concept of safe injection sites, places where drug users can consume pre-obtained drugs under medical supervision. Such initiatives aim to reduce the risks of overdose, spread of infectious diseases, and public drug use, while also linking users with health care services and treatment options.

Rehabilitation and counseling services are also increasingly seen as crucial pillars in addressing the intertwined challenges of substance abuse and homelessness. Instead of shunning those with addiction issues, progressive policies now aim to embrace them, understanding their histories, the triggers for their dependencies, and helping them forge a path to recovery.

Providing platforms where individuals can reconnect with society, gain vocational skills, and rebuild their self-worth is paramount.

After all, substance abuse, at its core, often stems from a profound sense of disconnection and pain. Addressing this root cause, offering acceptance and understanding, and integrating harm reduction strategies into the fabric of societal response can pave the way for a more holistic and compassionate approach to the complex dance between substance abuse and homelessness.

The Poverty Conundrum

Poverty, often seen as the root cause of many societal issues, acts as the underbelly of homelessness. While homelessness might manifest as a visible symptom, poverty operates in the shadows, a silent machinery propelling individuals and families towards precarious living situations.

In our rapidly globalizing world, cities and towns are seeing explosive growth. Real estate prices soar, and gentrification pushes lower-income communities further to the margins. In such urban landscapes, affordable housing becomes increasingly scarce, and many are priced out of their own neighborhoods. Without adequate and affordable housing options, families and individuals living paycheck to paycheck are perpetually one crisis away from the brink of homelessness.

Economic policies play a pivotal role in either mitigating or exacerbating these circumstances. For instance, regressive tax systems, where the burden disproportionately falls on the poorer segments of the population, can stifle economic mobility. On the other hand, progressive taxation, which places a larger tax responsibility on the wealthier, can generate funds to invest in social programs, public housing, and community development.

However, housing alone isn't the panacea. A comprehensive approach recognizes that intertwined with housing are other facets of life impacted by poverty.

Access to quality education, for instance, is a cornerstone of breaking the generational cycle of poverty. By ensuring that children from economically disadvantaged backgrounds receive the same educational opportunities as their affluent peers, societies lay the groundwork for upward mobility, reducing the risk of future homelessness.

Healthcare is another crucial dimension. In many countries, medical expenses are a leading cause of bankruptcy. A sudden illness or accident, without a robust healthcare safety net, can plunge families into debt, forcing them to make the untenable choice between medical care and a roof over their heads. Comprehensive health policies that prioritize preventive care, and provide safety nets for catastrophic health events, are essential in ensuring that medical emergencies don't translate into homelessness.

Access to stable employment opportunities is a significant factor. Vocational training, apprenticeship programs, and initiatives that support small businesses can provide avenues for consistent income, enabling individuals to not just escape the clutches of homelessness but to thrive.

The challenge of homelessness cannot be decoupled from the broader issue of poverty. Addressing homelessness in isolation, without confronting its economic underpinnings, offers only temporary relief. For a lasting solution, there's a need for a holistic approach that melds housing strategies with broader socio-economic reforms, knitting together a safety net that ensures every individual, regardless of their economic stature, has a place to call home.

The intricacies of homelessness stretch far beyond the immediate visuals of tents on sidewalks or people huddled in park benches. Each individual's journey into and through homelessness is unique, but many of these stories share underlying themes influenced by systemic failings, societal biases, and unforeseen personal tragedies. While the symptom might manifest as a lack of physical shelter, the underlying causes are woven into the very fabric of our societal structures, from our education systems to our healthcare provisions and our economic policies.

To truly address the issue of homelessness, it becomes paramount for policymakers to adopt a multi-dimensional perspective. This requires not only a comprehensive understanding of the factors that drive individuals into homelessness but also a profound commitment to addressing these root causes in tandem. Piecemeal solutions or singularly focused initiatives, while providing temporary relief, often fail to generate lasting impact.

Effective policymaking, therefore, needs a two-pronged approach. On one hand, immediate and urgent interventions are necessary to provide relief to those currently experiencing homelessness. This includes emergency shelters, food services, and medical aid. On the other hand, long-term strategies must be laid down to tackle the foundational issues leading to homelessness. These range from creating affordable housing projects and strengthening mental health support networks to implementing robust employment programs and ensuring universal access to quality education.

At the heart of these policies must be the voices of those directly affected. Incorporating the lived experiences of the homeless community provides valuable insights that can guide more empathetic and effective interventions.

By actively involving this community in the decision-making process, policies can be grounded in the realities of those they aim to serve. The path to eradicating homelessness is neither straightforward nor singular. It requires a mosaic of initiatives, policies, and collaborations that operate in harmony. While the challenge is undoubtedly vast, with informed, compassionate, and comprehensive strategies, societies can inch closer to a world where homelessness is an anomaly, not a recurring narrative.

Filling the Gaps: Policy Recommendations for the Future

Our approach to addressing homelessness must also adapt, learn, and innovate. Recognizing the gaps in existing policies and proactively strategizing for the future is a necessary endeavor for any government or organization committed to eradicating homelessness. Here are some policy recommendations to consider as we move forward:

A key component that often gets overlooked is the need for continuous research. Understanding the changing dynamics of homelessness, particularly as they relate to global phenomena like economic recessions, pandemics, or refugee crises, is essential. Governments and institutions should allocate resources to fund comprehensive studies that not only map the current scenario but also forecast potential future challenges. This proactive stance can help in designing preemptive strategies.

Another area of focus should be the integration of technology. Digital platforms can be utilized to connect homeless individuals with available resources, be it shelters, employment opportunities, or medical services. Furthermore, data analytics can help in tracking the effectiveness of existing programs, allowing for real-time tweaks and improvements.

While it's crucial to address the immediate needs of the homeless, an equal emphasis should be placed on prevention. This entails investing in educational programs, mental health initiatives, and economic stability projects that can reduce the risk factors associated with homelessness. By ensuring that citizens have a strong safety net, societies can prevent many from ever experiencing homelessness.

Creating channels for community involvement can be transformative. Engaging citizens in policymaking or in voluntary roles can foster a sense of collective responsibility. Community-led initiatives, from mentorship programs to skill-sharing workshops, can empower the homeless and provide them with tools to rebuild their lives.

There's an urgent need to decriminalize homelessness. Instead of punitive measures, the emphasis should be on rehabilitation and support. Law enforcement agencies should be trained to adopt a compassionate approach, connecting the homeless with social services rather than penalizing them.

As we look to the future, the emphasis should shift from mere management of the homelessness crisis to its complete eradication. This requires a holistic, inclusive, and forward-thinking approach that combines the best of policymaking, community engagement, and technological innovation. It's a formidable task but one that holds the promise of building societies where every individual is assured of dignity, safety, and opportunity.

When considering the profound complexities surrounding homelessness, a deeper analysis reveals layers of societal, economic, and personal intersections that contribute to its perpetuation. Hence, when formulating policy recommendations for the future, it's not just about filling the gaps but also about reinventing the structural foundation from which these gaps arise.

Historically, many homelessness policies have been reactive – focusing on addressing the issue once it has manifested. However, a more profound understanding requires us to recognize and act upon the pre-existing vulnerabilities that often lead to homelessness. This involves considering the socio-economic systems in place, the socio-cultural narratives that influence perceptions, and the accessibility of resources for prevention and intervention.

For instance, housing markets worldwide have become increasingly volatile. Rapid urbanization, speculative real estate investments, and gentrification have made housing unaffordable for many. Therefore, future policies should not just aim at providing immediate shelter but should also focus on stabilizing housing markets, regulating rent controls, and ensuring that urban development is inclusive. Urban planning should prioritize affordable housing units and protect tenants from abrupt evictions.

Education and awareness stand as pivotal tools. Societal perceptions of homelessness, often marred by stereotypes and misconceptions, can hinder effective interventions. By integrating homelessness education into school curriculums and public campaigns, societies can foster empathy and facilitate a culture of active involvement. When communities understand the root causes and the lived realities of homeless individuals, they are more likely to support policies and initiatives aimed at assistance and prevention.

There's a pressing need to integrate multidisciplinary approaches. Mental health professionals, economists, sociologists, urban planners, and legal experts should collaborate to design policies. This interdisciplinary approach ensures a more holistic understanding and can lead to solutions that consider every facet of the issue.

Direct engagement with those who've experienced homelessness is essential. Their insights, often overlooked in high-level policy discussions, can shed light on ground realities, challenges, and potential solutions that might not be evident from a purely administrative standpoint.

International cooperation is of paramount importance. Homelessness, in its many manifestations, is a global challenge. Sharing best practices, collaborative research, joint funding for innovative solutions, and creating global platforms to discuss homelessness can pave the way for unified strategies that have broader impacts.

In synthesizing these deeper insights, it becomes clear that addressing homelessness in the future is less about isolated interventions and more about restructuring societal systems to be inclusive, empathetic, and proactive. It's a vision that challenges the status quo but is rooted in the belief of a world where every individual has a place, they can call home.

As we pierce the layers of homelessness and its intertwined challenges, it becomes evident that true resolution lies not only in policies but in a paradigm shift in societal values, systems, and structures.

Addressing homelessness at its core demands a transformation in our global psyche, one that transcends traditional methodologies and taps into the bedrock of collective human conscience.

When considering the nexus between homelessness and the systems in place, one must recognize that modern economies, often geared towards relentless growth, may inadvertently be exacerbating disparities. The trickle-down economic theory, which has been the backbone of many capitalist societies, promises that as the rich get richer, benefits will eventually flow down to the less affluent. However, this hasn't been universally realized. To genuinely address homelessness, the global economic model must pivot towards inclusive growth, ensuring that prosperity isn't just concentrated at the top but is equitably distributed.

The relationship between public spaces and homelessness needs reevaluation. Urban spaces, traditionally seen as growth epicenters, have frequently sidelined marginalized communities.

Modern cities need to adopt an ethos of 'shared spaces,' recognizing that every citizen, regardless of their economic status, has an equal claim to the city's resources, services, and spaces. Redefining public space utilization to ensure it benefits all can change the narrative around homelessness.

Technological advancements, while promising unprecedented growth, also bring forth challenges. The rise of automation threatens job markets, potentially pushing more into economic vulnerabilities. Policies must anticipate these shifts, ensuring that as technology advances, safety nets are fortified, skill adaptation is encouraged, and no one is left behind in the march of progress.

Culturally, there's a need for introspection. The stigmatization of homelessness is deep-seated in many societies, perpetuating a cycle of neglect and isolation. To counteract this, cultural and media outlets should be leveraged to humanize the homeless narrative, showcasing stories of resilience, dreams, and the inherent human desire for belonging.

Environmental factors, often overlooked, also play a role. With climate change leading to increased natural disasters, many are left displaced, inching towards homelessness. A commitment to sustainable environmental policies is thus indirectly a commitment to preventing potential homelessness.

A decentralized approach to policymaking can be invaluable. Local communities have a nuanced understanding of their specific challenges and can offer tailored solutions. Empowering local bodies, NGOs, and community leaders to have a more significant say in policy decisions can lead to more effective, grounded strategies.

Eradicating homelessness demands a multi-pronged, deeply introspective approach, one that doesn't just patch the cracks but rebuilds the entire edifice on pillars of empathy, inclusivity, and forward-thinking.

It's a journey that challenges every facet of modern society but promises a future anchored in genuine equity and shared humanity.

Chapter 6: Homelessness Prevention and Early Intervention Strategies

Navigating the intricate challenge of homelessness demands not just remedial solutions for those already ensnared by its grasp, but also a dedicated focus on its prevention. Drawing inspiration from the age-old wisdom that prevention often outweighs the remedy, it becomes evident that comprehensive strategies targeted at the root causes of homelessness can drastically reshape its trajectory. Rather than viewing homelessness as an inevitable societal ailment, envisioning a world where its onset is preempted forms the crux of innovative approaches in modern policymaking.

This chapter delves deep into the multifaceted approaches towards homelessness prevention. By casting a spotlight on proactive measures that fortify the foundations of society—education, employment, and healthcare—we begin to see a tapestry of interwoven strategies aimed at building resilience against the onset of homelessness. Moreover, the chapter evaluates the effectiveness and transformative potential of intervention mechanisms, such as diversion programs and rapid rehousing. These strategies, though varied, converge on a single aim: minimizing the risk factors that precipitate homelessness.

As we journey through this chapter, we'll journey across continents to glean insights from global models that have successfully redefined the narrative. From cities that have pioneered prevention-based paradigms to communities that have transformed the lives of their most vulnerable members through early interventions, this chapter serves as both an exposition and an inspiration.

Engage with us in this comprehensive exploration, as we not only aim to understand but also to underscore the power of foresight, innovation, and human-centric strategies in curbing homelessness before it takes root.

Proactive Measures: Education, Employment, and Healthcare

The ripple effect of foundational societal elements like education, employment, and healthcare on the landscape of homelessness is profound. Each of these facets, when fortified, acts as a bulwark against the vulnerabilities that may lead to homelessness. By understanding their interplay and significance, we can create a more proactive approach to tackling and preventing homelessness.

Education

The bedrock of societal growth, education offers more than just academic knowledge; it provides individuals with a gateway to upward mobility. The impacts of education reverberate beyond the classroom, influencing various facets of an individual's life. When people are armed with education, they have a wider array of opportunities available to them, allowing for greater financial stability and self-sufficiency.

The transformative power of education extends to shaping one's worldview and fostering a sense of community and belonging. With education, individuals can engage more actively in civic matters, participate in community development, and contribute positively to societal advancement. This heightened level of engagement not only enriches one's life but also strengthens community ties, creating a safety net against the isolating experience of homelessness.

Education is a crucial tool in breaking generational cycles of poverty and homelessness. Children from families that have experienced homelessness stand at a higher risk of facing similar challenges in adulthood. However, with access to quality education, these children can rewrite their narratives, positioning themselves for brighter futures.

The pathway to education is not without its barriers. Socio-economic disparities, systemic prejudices, and a lack of resources can impede access to quality education for many. This makes it imperative for policymakers and community leaders to focus on leveling the playing field. Efforts should be directed towards ensuring that everyone, regardless of their socio-economic background, has equal access to education. This includes providing adequate resources, creating inclusive curricula that reflect diverse experiences, and implementing support systems for students facing challenges outside the classroom.

In the fight against homelessness, education serves as a linchpin, linking personal growth with societal progress. By prioritizing education and ensuring its universal accessibility, we can create a society where homelessness becomes a diminishing challenge, and a brighter future becomes a tangible reality for all.

Highlights for Education, Employment, and Healthcare

Education: A strong educational foundation is a powerful antidote against poverty and instability. Quality education equips individuals with skills, knowledge, and confidence, thereby increasing their employability and resilience against economic shocks. Moreover, education empowers individuals with critical thinking and problem-solving abilities, allowing them to better navigate the challenges of life. It's no surprise that there's a strong correlation between higher levels of education and lower rates of homelessness. However, this also underscores the importance of ensuring that educational institutions are accessible, inclusive, and equipped to support students from all backgrounds, particularly those at risk.

Employment: Stable employment is often the cornerstone of economic independence. Without a consistent source of income, individuals and families can rapidly descend into financial instability, making them susceptible to homelessness. Furthermore, employment isn't merely a financial proposition; it also offers a sense of purpose, identity, and social connection. Policies and programs that focus on job training, skill development, and ensuring a fair wage can play a significant role in keeping people housed. On the flip side, addressing barriers to employment—be it discrimination, lack of childcare, or gaps in work history due to homelessness—is equally pivotal.

Healthcare: The nexus between healthcare and homelessness is multifaceted. Without access to adequate healthcare, medical emergencies can quickly spiral into financial crises. Moreover, chronic health conditions, if not managed, can lead to job losses or prolonged absences, pushing individuals further into the abyss of economic instability. Mental health, often overlooked, plays a significant role too. Without access to timely interventions and support, those grappling with mental health challenges might find the path to stable housing riddled with obstacles.

Employment

Beyond the obvious monetary gains, employment plays a vital role in shaping an individual's self-worth and place in society. A job is more than just a means to an end; it serves as a platform for personal growth, interaction, and societal contribution. The security that comes from a regular paycheck goes hand in hand with the emotional and psychological benefits derived from being a productive member of the community.

The ripple effects of stable employment touch various aspects of life. For instance, it allows individuals to access better healthcare, engage in recreational activities, and even plan for future endeavors such as higher education or homeownership. Furthermore, the workplace itself becomes a hub of social interaction, where friendships are forged and support systems built, which can be pivotal during challenging times.

The journey to stable employment is riddled with challenges for many. Those reentering the job market after a bout of homelessness often find themselves at a disadvantage, having to explain gaps in their employment history. Others might face challenges due to limited education or outdated skill sets. Furthermore, societal prejudices can act as invisible barriers, particularly for marginalized groups.

It is imperative for governments, businesses, and community organizations to come together in creating an employment ecosystem that is inclusive and supportive. This could mean establishing mentorship programs, offering on-the-job training, or even creating platforms where individuals can learn new, market-relevant skills. Beyond this, creating a work environment that respects diversity and promotes inclusivity can also make a significant difference.

Employment acts as both a protective shield against homelessness and a ladder towards socio-economic growth. By focusing on comprehensive employment strategies that are rooted in inclusivity and empowerment, we can create a robust mechanism that not only prevents homelessness but also ensures a more equitable society for all.

Healthcare

An individual's well-being is intrinsically tied to their access to quality healthcare. The intricate dance between one's health and their socio-economic status is evident in how medical setbacks can exacerbate financial vulnerabilities. An unexpected medical ailment, in the absence of adequate healthcare coverage, can become the initial domino that sets off a cascade of hardships, from accumulating medical debts to the inability to continue working.

But healthcare isn't solely about treating physical ailments. It encapsulates a holistic understanding of well-being, including mental and emotional health. For many, the lack of proper mental health support can lead to a cyclical pattern where the challenges of homelessness exacerbate mental health issues, which in turn make it harder to escape homelessness. Recognizing and addressing mental health as an integral component of overall health is paramount.

Preventive healthcare measures can serve as a buffer. Regular check-ups, health education, and early interventions can reduce the risk of severe health issues that might otherwise lead to job losses or debilitating expenses. Access to reproductive health services, nutritional guidance, and substance abuse treatment centers further underscores the breadth of healthcare's role in preventing homelessness.

In a rapidly evolving world, where health challenges range from pandemics to the rise in non-communicable diseases, it becomes all the more crucial for societies to prioritize universal healthcare access. A proactive and inclusive healthcare system, which addresses the varied needs of its populace, becomes a foundational pillar in the architecture of a society where homelessness is rare, brief, and non-recurring.

When viewed in isolation, education, employment, and healthcare each play a monumental role in the fabric of society.

However, in the context of homelessness prevention, their intertwined nature becomes even more evident.

These pillars do not operate in silos; instead, they influence and bolster each other. A well-educated individual stands a better chance at stable employment. Simultaneously, a gainfully employed individual can better access quality healthcare, and good health, in turn, enhances one's ability to learn and work efficiently.

It is this intricate web of dependencies and influences that underscores the need for a holistic approach. Addressing one without the others may offer only transient relief. The goal, therefore, is to create a societal structure where these proactive measures are not just available but are also synergistically linked, laying the groundwork for a comprehensive shield against homelessness.

Diversion Programs and Rapid Rehousing: Do They Work?

In the tapestry of solutions aimed at addressing homelessness, two approaches that have garnered significant attention in recent years are Diversion Programs and Rapid Rehousing. Both focus on reducing the time an individual or family spends homeless or preventing homelessness entirely. But how effective are these approaches? Let's delve deeper.

Diversion Programs are interventions that prevent homelessness at the onset. Before an individual or family enters a shelter or experiences homelessness, diversion efforts aim to find immediate alternate solutions. This can be through mediation with landlords, providing one-time financial assistance, or leveraging community networks to find temporary housing. The essence of diversion is to identify and harness resources before someone is on the streets. One of the hallmarks of this approach is its emphasis on dialogue. By conducting solution-oriented interviews, service providers assist those at risk of homelessness in brainstorming practical alternatives.

Diversion Programs stand at the frontline in the battle against homelessness, addressing the issue even before it manifests. These proactive strategies intercept potential crises, offering timely interventions to individuals or families teetering on the edge of displacement. By initiating crucial conversations with those at risk, these programs explore a myriad of tailored solutions. Engaging with landlords can sometimes resolve misunderstandings or offer extensions to payment deadlines.

In instances where financial hurdles are temporary, the provision of short-term monetary assistance can bridge the gap, preventing an eviction. Moreover, tapping into robust community ties can result in finding suitable accommodations, often sidestepping the need for shelters. An essential facet of these programs is their collaborative nature; they emphasize active participation from those seeking assistance, fostering a sense of agency and empowerment. The central idea is not just to provide a stopgap but to collaboratively chart a sustainable path forward, averting the immediate crisis of homelessness.

In many regions, diversion has demonstrated efficacy by reducing the inflow into the homeless service system. By curbing the number of people entering shelters, these programs ensure that shelters and other resources can focus on those who have no other alternatives.

Rapid Rehousing, on the other hand, operates on a simple premise: get individuals and families into stable housing as quickly as possible. Instead of prolonged stays in shelters or transitional housing, the focus is on immediate, permanent housing. This approach often comes coupled with time-limited financial assistance and case management services. The idea is that with a stable roof over one's head, it becomes easier to address other challenges, be it finding employment, accessing healthcare, or reconnecting with community networks.

Rapid Rehousing emerges from the understanding that a secure living environment is foundational to individual and familial well-being. By prioritizing swift transitions from precarious situations or shelters into permanent residences, this approach underscores the importance of stability in driving positive outcomes. Rather than letting individuals or families languish in interim solutions, Rapid Rehousing propels them towards self-sufficiency in their own homes.

Along with providing this immediate sanctuary, there's an infusion of tailored support mechanisms. While the financial scaffolding, often temporary, aids in smoothing out initial resettling processes, the embedded case management services are indispensable. These services holistically address multifaceted needs, ensuring that once rehoused, individuals have the necessary tools and guidance to rebuild and thrive. By intertwining housing with essential supports, this approach not only remedies the immediate housing crisis but also lays the groundwork for long-term resilience and prosperity.

The success of Rapid Rehousing is evident in the shorter spells of homelessness and decreased returns to homelessness. By reducing the trauma and upheaval associated with prolonged periods without stable housing, individuals and families are better positioned to rebuild their lives.

While both Diversion Programs and Rapid Rehousing show promise, they are not without challenges. Adequate funding, the availability of affordable housing, and community buy-in are essential for these models to thrive. Moreover, these approaches must be part of a larger ecosystem of services, from preventive measures to support for those with chronic homelessness experiences.

Diversion Programs and Rapid Rehousing offer promising avenues in the battle against homelessness, however, their efficacy hinges on their integration into a broader strategy, addressing the root causes and systemic challenges that precipitate homelessness.

Preventive Models from Around the World

Tackling homelessness requires foresight, innovation, and an emphasis on proactive measures. Recognizing that the best way to combat homelessness is to prevent its occurrence in the first place, many regions worldwide have shifted their focus from reactive measures to prevention and early intervention. By anticipating potential triggers and acting early, it's possible to reduce the overall number of people experiencing homelessness and minimize the adverse effects on individuals and communities.

From the bustling streets of Tokyo to the vibrant neighborhoods of Bogotá, diverse strategies rooted in prevention have emerged, each reflecting the unique socio-cultural and economic dynamics of its region. As we traverse the globe in our exploration, we'll uncover a tapestry of preventive models, each with its own story of challenge, innovation, and hope. These case studies not only highlight the importance of a preemptive approach but also underscore the power of community, collaboration, and commitment in crafting solutions that are both impactful and sustainable.

Toronto, Canada

In Canada's most populous city, the "Streets to Homes" program stands out as an innovative approach to addressing homelessness. The initiative focuses on outreach, where teams actively engage with individuals living on the streets. Rather than pushing for immediate shelter entry, the program's goal is to transition people directly into permanent housing. Once housed, individuals receive a range of supports tailored to their needs, from employment assistance to health services.

Copenhagen, Denmark

As part of Denmark's national strategy to combat homelessness, Copenhagen launched the "Housing First" model. Echoing its name, the program's primary principle is that stable housing should be the initial step in assisting those experiencing homelessness. By offering housing without preconditions, such as sobriety, the model acknowledges the complexities of homelessness and prioritizes stability over behavioral mandates. This progressive stance has led to remarkable success rates in keeping participants housed and connected to necessary support services.

Wellington, New Zealand

The "Te Mahana" strategy in Wellington is a testament to a community-driven approach to homelessness prevention. Leveraging a strong collaboration between government agencies, NGOs, and local Maori communities, the strategy is rooted in a vision of inclusive cities where everyone belongs. Central to its ethos is the belief in early intervention, ensuring that those at risk of homelessness receive timely support, be it financial counseling, mental health services, or addiction treatment.

Bangalore, India

In one of India's bustling tech hubs, a unique model, "Shelter and Skills," was birthed. Recognizing that shelter alone is not enough, the initiative intertwines housing with vocational training. Individuals are not only given a safe space to reside but are also equipped with skills, from carpentry to computer programming, ensuring they have a viable path to economic independence.

São Paulo, Brazil

The "Teto e Trabalho" (Roof and Work) program illustrates how cities can be innovative even with limited resources. São Paulo's municipal government partners with local businesses to create employment opportunities specifically for those transitioning out of homelessness. In tandem with job placements, participants are provided with housing subsidies, ensuring they have both a livelihood and a home.

These case studies, though diverse in their approaches, underscore a shared understanding that prevention and early intervention are pivotal in the fight against homelessness. By offering models that are proactive rather than reactive, cities around the world are showcasing that with ingenuity, collaboration, and commitment, homelessness can be not just managed but substantially reduced.

Chapter 7: Homelessness and Social Justice

Homelessness is not merely an economic or policy issue; it is intrinsically tied to broader themes of social justice, equity, and human rights. As we delve into the nexus between homelessness and societal structures, it becomes increasingly clear that homelessness isn't a standalone phenomenon but is deeply interwoven with systemic inequities that exist in our societies. These inequities disproportionately affect marginalized communities, amplifying the challenges they face and placing them at a higher risk of experiencing homelessness.

The nuances and layers within marginalized communities bring to the fore the complexities of homelessness. Discrimination based on race, ethnicity, gender, sexuality, disability, and other identity markers can compound economic vulnerabilities. It becomes not just a struggle for shelter but a battle against deeply ingrained prejudices and structural barriers that have been erected over generations.

This chapter is not just an exploration of challenges; it's a journey into solutions, resilience, and change. By shedding light on systemic inequities, we hope to chart a path forward that's inclusive, just, and transformative. Recognizing these challenges is the first step, but the true testament of progress lies in how societies and systems respond. Through advocacy, awareness campaigns, and the relentless efforts of grassroots movements, we witness the power of collective action. These stories serve as a reminder that change is not only possible but is happening, powered by communities and individuals dedicated to creating a more just and equitable world.

As we navigate through this chapter, we invite readers to view homelessness through the lens of social justice. By doing so, we gain a holistic understanding of its root causes, its manifestations, and, most importantly, the collaborative efforts required to address it. Through shared knowledge, empathy, and activism, we can challenge the status quo, pushing for reforms and solutions that prioritize dignity, rights, and social justice for all.

The Magnified Impact on Marginalized Communities

For many marginalized communities, the threat of homelessness is not an abstract or distant concept; it's an ever-present reality, exacerbated by systemic barriers that have persisted for generations. Discrimination, lack of representation, and societal biases have cumulatively created environments where certain groups are more vulnerable to homelessness than others.

Indigenous Communities and Homelessness

Indigenous communities across the globe hold a unique position in history, often recognized as the original inhabitants of lands that later underwent colonization, development, and modernization. Their diverse narratives converge around themes of displacement, cultural erosion, and systemic marginalization.

To comprehend the homelessness faced by many indigenous peoples today, one must delve into the historical injustices they've endured. Colonial conquests, broken treaties, forced assimilations, and, in certain regions, residential schools have systematically undermined their way of life. These acts did more than deprive them of land; they often aimed to erase their cultural, spiritual, and communal identities.

As cities and urban centers expanded, indigenous communities frequently experienced pushback to the outskirts or faced complete displacement. Such movements weren't merely geographical shifts. They disrupted community structures, inter-generational learning, and ties to ancestral lands, which are integral to many indigenous identities.

In these urban environments, the dual challenge of integrating into the mainstream, while simultaneously preserving a unique cultural identity, emerged prominently.

Despite proximity to urban centers, many indigenous communities remain deprived of equal access to modern amenities. The systemic discrimination they face is evident in areas like education, with unequal funding for indigenous schools, subpar healthcare facilities, and limited employment opportunities. Such disparities are not just material in nature but indicate a broader societal neglect of the value of indigenous lives and their contributions.

Land for many indigenous individuals isn't merely a physical entity. It's deeply connected with spirituality, culture, and history. Separation from these ancestral territories signifies not just a loss of habitat but also a disconnection from identity, history, and spirituality. The compounded trauma of such disconnection, alongside daily adversities, can lead to profound psychological impacts.

Though some regions have attempted to redress historical injustices through mechanisms like land settlements, reparations, or recognition of indigenous rights, these often don't alleviate the immediate challenges indigenous communities face. True redress demands a comprehensive approach, one that doesn't only rectify past wrongs but also addresses ongoing inequities, ensuring that indigenous communities are respected, equipped, and empowered for the future.

In addressing homelessness within indigenous communities, it's paramount that strategies are rooted in an understanding of their unique histories, values, and aspirations. Solutions devoid of this insight risk being not only ineffective but potentially detrimental.

LGBTQ+ Individuals and the Quest for Acceptance and Stability

LGBTQ+ individuals frequently find themselves navigating a world that oscillates between acceptance and prejudice. For many, the very act of embracing their authentic self comes with dire consequences, with familial rejection being one of the most heart-wrenching. When family, the primary unit of social support, turns its back, the world can seem unforgiving.

For young LGBTQ+ individuals, this rejection is especially calamitous. Adolescence and young adulthood are already phases characterized by self-discovery and the quest for autonomy.

When LGBTQ+ youth are rejected by their families, they are robbed of the safety nets many of their peers take for granted. Without emotional and financial support, basic needs like housing, education, and sustenance become monumental challenges. Many find themselves in precarious living situations or are forced to resort to survival tactics, some of which can be detrimental to their well-being.

The external world isn't always more welcoming. Despite progress in LGBTQ+ rights in various regions, discrimination persists. Housing discrimination, for instance, is a palpable reality for many. Landlords, either due to personal prejudices or societal pressures, may be reluctant to rent to LGBTQ+ individuals, especially if they don't conform to traditional gender presentations. The consequence? A lack of safe and affirming spaces where they can rebuild their lives.

The professional realm isn't devoid of these challenges either. Discrimination in employment can manifest in many ways – from outright rejection based on sexual orientation or gender identity to subtler forms like microaggressions, limited career advancement, or lack of adequate workplace protections. Such challenges not only affect their economic stability but can also erode self-esteem and mental well-being.

The trauma and stress of navigating a world riddled with prejudice leave scars. Mental health disparities in the LGBTQ+ community, when compared to their heterosexual counterparts, are significant. The need for mental health services and support is paramount, but many regions lack specialized care that understands and respects LGBTQ+ experiences.

It's essential to note that the story of LGBTQ+ individuals isn't solely one of adversity. Across the world, they've showcased remarkable resilience, forging communities of acceptance, leading movements for rights, and carving out spaces where they can celebrate their authentic selves. Still, it remains a societal obligation to ensure that no one has to face homelessness or marginalization simply for being true to who they are.

Migrants and Refugees: Navigating a World Away from Home

In an age where geopolitical tensions, economic disparities, and climate change propel the movement of people across borders, migrants and refugees stand as some of the most vulnerable groups. Their journey from the familiar terrains of home to lands unknown is not merely geographic; it's a complex maze of emotional, economic, and sociocultural transitions.

Beginning with their reasons for migration, every refugee or migrant carries a tapestry of stories. Whether they're escaping the horrors of war, the iron grip of persecution, or the jaws of economic destitution, their departure is rarely ever a matter of choice.

They leave behind homes, memories, and a significant part of their identity. However, the promise of safety or a better life, though compelling, doesn't always translate into an easy transition.

Upon arrival in new countries, the initial relief often gives way to an array of challenges. The most immediate among these is shelter. With limited resources at their disposal and, at times, large families to care for, securing stable housing can be a significant hurdle. Temporary camps, often the first point of refuge, can become long-term dwelling places, lacking in basic amenities and privacy.

Language acts as another formidable barrier. Without proficiency in the local language, everyday tasks become daunting. From accessing services to seeking employment, the lack of linguistic capabilities can exacerbate feelings of isolation and impede integration. This can also limit their understanding of their rights and available resources, making them more susceptible to misinformation.

Cultural assimilation, too, is a nuanced journey. Migrants and refugees, bringing with them rich traditions and experiences, might find it challenging to navigate the cultural mores of their new homes. This can affect their social interactions, making community integration a prolonged process.

Legal constraints further complicate their plight. Depending on their status, migrants and refugees might find doors closed at multiple junctures. Some may be restricted from formal employment sectors, pushing them into underpaid or exploitative jobs. Others, especially those without proper documentation, live under constant fear of deportation. This fear, often valid, discourages many from seeking help even when faced with dire situations, including homelessness or exploitation.

It's worth noting that despite these challenges, migrants and refugees exhibit remarkable resilience and determination. Their contributions to the cultural, social, and economic fabric of their adopted countries are substantial.

Their vulnerability, especially in the initial stages of their transition, necessitates a more empathetic, inclusive, and supportive approach from host countries and communities. Addressing their unique challenges isn't merely a humanitarian act; it's a step towards building diverse, enriched, and harmonious societies.

Persons with Disabilities: Navigating Barriers in a Non-Inclusive World

The journey of persons with disabilities is riddled with unique challenges that are often overlooked by the majority. Their experiences are not just about physical limitations but encompass a broader spectrum of socio-cultural and systemic barriers. For many, the world isn't just a place to navigate, but a continuous puzzle that often lacks the necessary pieces to fit their distinct needs.

At the heart of the matter is the overarching theme of inclusivity—or more accurately, the lack of it. Societies worldwide, despite advancements, frequently fall short in offering genuinely inclusive environments. These shortcomings manifest in various forms, ranging from architectural barriers to prejudiced attitudes.

Housing is a fundamental aspect where these disparities are glaringly apparent. Accessible housing, tailored to cater to specific physical needs, is not as readily available as one might assume. Many residential areas lack basic modifications, such as ramps, elevators, or sensory aids, making them inhospitable to those with mobility or sensory impairments. The limited availability of such housing often translates to higher costs, pushing it out of reach for many with disabilities, especially when compounded with limited earning opportunities.

Education and employment, two crucial pillars for stability, present their sets of challenges. Despite policies advocating for inclusive education, the ground realities often differ. Schools and institutions might lack the necessary infrastructure or trained personnel to cater to diverse learning needs. This lack of early educational support can have ripple effects, limiting higher education and subsequently, employment opportunities.

The employment landscape, too, is riddled with biases. Persons with disabilities frequently face discriminatory attitudes during hiring processes. Employers, often driven by misconceptions, might overlook the capabilities of disabled individuals, focusing instead on their limitations. This systemic discrimination results in lower employment rates, limited career growth, and consequently, economic instability.

Societal attitudes play a significant role in the challenges faced by persons with disabilities. Stereotypes and biases can lead to social isolation. Such isolation not only affects mental well-being but can also limit access to community support networks, essential for navigating life's challenges.

For persons with disabilities, the pathway to stable housing and a consistent life is layered with barriers that go beyond their physical challenges. These barriers, systemic in nature, require a multi-pronged approach to dismantle. Societies must move beyond mere tokenistic measures and invest in creating environments where inclusivity isn't an afterthought but a foundational principle. Only then can the risk of homelessness among persons with disabilities be genuinely mitigated.

Women Facing Domestic Abuse: The Intersection of Safety and Shelter

The perilous journey of women ensnared in the vicious cycle of domestic abuse is a testament to the myriad ways homelessness can manifest. It underscores that not all pathways to homelessness are paved with economic woes. Sometimes, it's the desperate search for safety and dignity that propels one into the harrowing embrace of homelessness.

Domestic abuse is, unfortunately, a pervasive issue that transcends geographical boundaries, cultures, and socio-economic classes. The patterns of abuse might vary, but the underlying theme remains consistent: power and control. For the victims, often women, but also including men and members of the LGBTQ+ community, this translates into a daily life of fear, manipulation, and continuous degradation.

For many, the idea of leaving such an environment seems like the obvious solution. Yet, the reality is much more convoluted. The decision to walk away from an abusive household isn't solely about mustering the courage; it's intricately tied to the availability of alternatives. Without a secure place to retreat to, the decision becomes fraught with uncertainties. Can they find shelter? Will they have the resources to sustain themselves? And crucially, will they be safe from their abusers?

Shelters designated for victims of domestic abuse are a beacon of hope. However, their availability is often limited, and they might be overwhelmed by the sheer volume of those in need. Even when they are available, concerns about confidentiality, duration of stay, and the well-being of children (if any) can pose barriers.

Economic dependency plays a significant role. Abusers often exert control by restricting access to financial resources, leaving the victim economically tethered. In such scenarios, the prospect of leaving becomes even more daunting. Where will they go? How will they support themselves or their children? These pressing questions, coupled with the genuine fear of retribution, make the pathway out of an abusive household a labyrinthine challenge.

Then there's the psychological dimension. Years of abuse can erode self-worth and confidence, making the idea of starting afresh seem insurmountable. The societal stigma attached to domestic abuse, and sometimes misplaced blame on the victim, further compounds the issue.

To truly support victims of domestic abuse and reduce their risk of homelessness, there's a need for a holistic approach. This involves not just increasing the availability of shelters but also providing comprehensive support, from legal assistance and counseling to job training and childcare. Moreover, societal attitudes need a shift: from victim-blaming to empowering, from turning a blind eye to actively creating support networks.

It's crucial to understand that for these marginalized communities, homelessness is often the culmination of a series of systemic failures. Their experiences are not just shaped by their immediate circumstances but by historical injustices, discriminatory policies, and societal neglect. By addressing the unique challenges faced by these groups, we can begin to craft solutions that are tailored, effective, and sustainable.

Addressing Systemic Inequities: A Path Forward

At the crossroads of homelessness and social justice lies a landscape marred by systemic inequities. To view homelessness merely as a product of individual circumstances is a gross oversimplification. Beneath the surface, the roots of homelessness often intertwine with larger systemic issues— structural biases, historical marginalization, and entrenched socio-economic disparities. Addressing homelessness, therefore, demands not just reactive measures but a proactive dismantling of these systemic barriers.

Historical Context and Ongoing Ramifications

Every society carries the weight of its historical baggage. Colonial legacies, racial segregation, discriminatory laws, and socio-political unrest have left indelible marks on the societal fabric. These histories have led to generations of marginalized communities being economically disadvantaged, lacking access to quality education, housing, and job opportunities. Recognizing and rectifying the ongoing impacts of such historical injustices is paramount. It involves policies that are restorative in nature, focusing on not just equality but also equity.

Economic Restructuring for Fairness

Economic policies often play a pivotal role in either amplifying or reducing systemic inequities. Regressive taxation, for instance, can further entrench wealth disparities, pushing vulnerable populations closer to the brink of homelessness. A forward-looking strategy would involve crafting policies that ensure fair wage practices, bolster social safety nets, and prioritize affordable housing initiatives. By making economies work for everyone, rather than a privileged few, the spiral into homelessness can be curtailed.

Policy Reforms with Intersectionality at the Forefront

Every individual's experience is shaped by the intersection of their various identities—be it race, gender, sexual orientation, or disability. Policies that do not account for this complex interplay are bound to have blind spots. A path forward involves adopting an intersectional lens, where policies are designed with a nuanced understanding of these overlapping identities. This would lead to more comprehensive and inclusive solutions, reducing the risk of certain groups falling through the cracks.

Strengthening Community Cohesion

At the heart of systemic change lies the power of community. Communities that are tightly knit, where members are vigilant about each other's welfare, can act as a bulwark against homelessness. Initiatives that foster community bonding, promote cultural understanding, and encourage neighborhood inclusivity can be instrumental. When individuals feel a sense of belonging, they are better positioned to access community resources and support during times of crisis.

Collaborative Approaches for Greater Impact

Addressing systemic inequities is not the sole responsibility of any single entity. It requires the collective efforts of governments, non-profits, businesses, and civil society. By fostering multi-stakeholder collaborations, pooling resources, and sharing expertise, the fight against systemic roots of homelessness can be invigorated.

The path forward is not just about building more shelters or creating short-term interventions. It's about reshaping societies—making them more just, inclusive, and equitable. Only by confronting and dismantling the systemic barriers that push individuals into homelessness can lasting solutions be found.

Advocacy, Awareness Campaigns, and Grassroots Movements: Powering Change

The battle against homelessness and the pursuit of social justice are often fought in the corridors of power, but their true momentum is generated on the streets, in community centers, and through digital campaigns that mobilize masses. Advocacy, awareness campaigns, and grassroots movements have historically been, and continue to be, the lifeblood of systemic change.

Advocacy efforts play a pivotal role in translating ground realities into actionable policy recommendations. Through persistent lobbying, representation, and dialogue with decision-makers, advocates ensure that the voices of the marginalized are not just heard but acted upon. They bridge the gap between communities and policymakers, making sure that solutions crafted in legislative halls resonate with the real needs of the people.

Awareness campaigns work wonders in shifting public perceptions. Homelessness, often shrouded in stereotypes and misconceptions, needs to be understood in its multifaceted complexity. Through documentaries, storytelling, art installations, and media coverage, these campaigns shed light on the human stories behind the statistics. By humanizing the issue, they garner empathy, challenge biases, and inspire collective action.

But perhaps the most potent force in this trinity is grassroots movements. Springing from the very heart of communities, these movements are grounded in lived experiences. They mobilize local resources, foster community cohesion, and act as first responders to emerging challenges. Whether it's a neighborhood group ensuring that vacant homes are made available to the homeless, a community kitchen serving meals to those in need, or local organizations offering skill development workshops, the grassroots impact is tangible and immediate.

In an age dominated by digital communication, grassroots movements have found new avenues to amplify their reach.

Social media campaigns, online petitions, and virtual town halls have democratized activism, allowing for a broader participation and global solidarity. These digital tools, when harnessed effectively, can escalate local issues to a global platform, garnering international support and resources.

In the broader tapestry of change, while policymakers, researchers, and NGOs play critical roles, it's often the advocates, the awareness campaigners, and the grassroots leaders who are at the forefront. They challenge the status quo, push boundaries, and inspire communities to take ownership of their collective futures. Through their relentless efforts, they not only highlight the urgent need for change but also demonstrate the possibilities that arise when communities come together in the spirit of solidarity and action.

In addressing homelessness through the lens of social justice, the nuance lies not just in the surface-level actions of advocates, campaigners, and grassroots leaders but in the foundational philosophies and methodologies they employ.

Each of these groups operates from a unique vantage point, and their effectiveness stems from their approach as much as their actions.

Advocates, for instance, often need to straddle two worlds. On one side, they interact with those facing the harsh realities of homelessness daily, and on the other, they engage with policymakers who operate within a framework of legislative and bureaucratic constraints. The nuanced art of advocacy is in synthesizing these two worlds. Effective advocates are not just empathetic listeners but also strategic communicators, able to distill complex, personal narratives into compelling arguments that resonate with policymakers. They recognize that true advocacy goes beyond just speaking for the marginalized; it's about empowering these communities to speak for themselves, ensuring their voices lead the discourse.

Awareness campaigns, meanwhile, face the challenge of overcoming an often apathetic or misinformed public perception. The depth of these campaigns is rooted in their ability to tap into the emotional core of the issue without oversimplifying or sensationalizing it. Effective campaigns not only present facts but also weave them into relatable narratives, making the distant issue of homelessness feel personal and immediate. They challenge societal norms, question long-held beliefs, and prompt individuals to confront their own biases. The measure of their success often isn't in the immediacy of their impact but in the lasting change in public discourse and consciousness they foster.

Grassroots movements, with their close proximity to the ground realities, inherently understand the complexities of local contexts. Their depth lies in their adaptability and responsiveness. Unlike top-down initiatives, grassroots movements are shaped by the communities they serve, ensuring that solutions are tailored to local needs, cultural nuances, and available resources. Their strength is derived from community ownership. It's not just about executing a project; it's about building capacity within the community, ensuring that the momentum of change is sustained long after specific interventions end. They foster a sense of local pride, resilience, and self-reliance, qualities essential for long-term transformation.

As these movements operate, they often unearth deeper systemic issues — be it discriminatory local policies, gaps in service delivery, or socio-cultural barriers.

By highlighting these challenges and mobilizing community-led solutions, grassroots initiatives play a crucial role in influencing broader systemic changes.

When delving deeper into the tapestry of social justice efforts around homelessness, it becomes evident that the synergy between advocates, awareness campaigns, and grassroots movements is not just complementary but profoundly interconnected. Their combined efforts create a holistic ecosystem of change, where insights from one domain inform actions in another, creating a ripple effect that has the potential to reshape societies.

In the multifaceted challenge that homelessness presents to societies worldwide, research stands as a beacon, illuminating the contours of the problem and guiding the formulation of evidence-based solutions. Through relentless inquiry, observation, and analysis, researchers strive to disentangle the complex web of causes, consequences, and correlations that surround homelessness. As we venture into this chapter, we will embark on an intellectual journey through the dynamic landscape of homelessness research, a realm that is continually evolving in response to both the changing nature of homelessness and the advances in research methodologies.

We'll first delve into the emerging trends in homelessness research. As societies transform and new challenges arise, research paradigms shift to address these novel complexities. These trends are not merely academic exercises; they are reflective of the changing realities on the ground, be it due to economic shifts, societal changes, or global phenomena like pandemics.

From there, we'll explore the innovations in research methodology that are reshaping how data on homelessness is collected and analyzed. The move from traditional field studies to virtual surveys exemplifies the adaptability of the research community and the leveraging of technology in understanding a historically elusive issue. In this age of digital transformation, how are researchers ensuring the accuracy, ethics, and comprehensiveness of their methods?

A significant portion of our exploration will focus on data gaps and the pivotal importance of longitudinal studies. These studies, which track subjects over extended periods, are invaluable in understanding the long-term trajectories of homeless individuals, offering insights into the cyclical nature of homelessness and the long-term impacts of interventions.

The chapter will pivot to examining the impact of policies. Beyond theoretical frameworks, how do these policies play out in the real world? Policy impact analysis provides a rigorous assessment, holding policymakers accountable and ensuring that interventions lead to tangible, positive outcomes.

In a world rife with uncertainties, the ability to forecast future trends becomes paramount. Through sophisticated simulation models, researchers are now better equipped than ever to predict the potential trajectories of homelessness, allowing societies to preemptively address emerging challenges.

Through this chapter, we aim to offer a panoramic view of the research landscape, emphasizing the symbiotic relationship between rigorous inquiry and effective intervention. For, in the quest to eradicate homelessness, knowledge is not just power— it's the compass that points the way forward.

Emerging Trends in Homelessness Research

Homelessness, as a societal issue, is as dynamic as the societies it affects. Over the years, its nature, causes, and manifestations have evolved, spurred by shifts in global economics, climate change, regional conflicts, health crises, and societal transformations. Consequently, research on homelessness has continually adapted, embracing new themes, perspectives, and methodologies to stay abreast of these changes. Here, we explore some of the emerging trends in homelessness research:

The Impact of Global Phenomena

Recent years have seen an increased focus on how global phenomena, such as climate change and pandemics, affect homelessness. For instance, researchers are probing the links between extreme weather events, forced migration, and resultant homelessness. The COVID-19 pandemic, too, has brought to the fore the vulnerabilities of homeless populations, driving research on its immediate and long-term effects on this demographic.

Youth Homelessness

While homelessness among adults has long been a focus, there's a growing interest in understanding youth homelessness. This research examines the unique causes, such as family breakdown or aging out of foster care, and the distinct challenges that homeless youth face, including higher vulnerability to exploitation or mental health issues.

The Interplay of Homelessness and Technology

As technology becomes increasingly integrated into everyday life, researchers are studying its impact on homelessness. This includes examining how technology can both alleviate and exacerbate the issue—such as the role of online platforms in finding shelter or employment, versus the digital divide that may further marginalize the homeless.

Intersectionality in Homelessness

Recognizing that homelessness doesn't occur in a vacuum, there's a growing emphasis on studying it from an intersectional perspective. This involves examining how factors like race, gender, sexual orientation, and disability intersect with homelessness, leading to compounded vulnerabilities.

Health and Homelessness

Beyond the evident concerns of exposure and nutrition, there's a burgeoning interest in understanding the broader health implications of homelessness. This includes mental health, the challenges of managing chronic illnesses without stable housing, and the healthcare system's role in either mitigating or perpetuating homelessness.

Housing First and Beyond

While the Housing First approach has gained traction worldwide, researchers are delving deeper into its long-term outcomes, scalability, and how it integrates with other support systems.

Criminalization of Homelessness

As some regions respond to homelessness with punitive measures, there's a growing body of research examining the ramifications of such approaches. This includes studies on the cycle of incarceration and homelessness, the legal and ethical implications, and the societal costs of criminalization versus supportive interventions.

Economic Models of Homelessness

Moving beyond sociological and anthropological perspectives, there's a rising trend in employing economic models to understand homelessness. This involves examining the cost-effectiveness of interventions, the economic impact of homelessness on cities, and the role of housing markets and employment trends.

Homelessness research is vast and continually expanding. These emerging trends reflect a deeper, more nuanced understanding of the issue, embracing its complexities and interconnectedness with other societal facets. As researchers continue to probe, challenge, and innovate, they lay the groundwork for more informed, effective interventions in the battle against homelessness.

Innovations in Methodology: From Field Studies to Virtual Surveys

Research into homelessness, paralleling the dynamic nature of the phenomenon, continuously adapts. As the contours of society, technology, and academia reshape, the ways we study and interpret homelessness transform in tandem. Motivated by the ambition to gather data in manners that are more precise, ethically sound, and exhaustive, a rich tapestry of innovative techniques has been woven.

Traditional field studies, which historically involved direct engagement with homeless populations, have undergone notable revamps. Ethnographic research today sees investigators embedding themselves more profoundly within communities. In some instances, researchers even experience the harsh realities of homelessness firsthand, offering them a raw and unparalleled insight into the daily hurdles and incredible resilience of those without homes.

Concurrently, the dawn of the digital age has ushered in novel research avenues. Virtual surveys, powered by the ubiquity of smartphones and the versatility of online platforms, promise a far-reaching grasp, often encompassing demographics that might elude conventional street counts or surveys centered around shelters. When meshed with geolocation specifics, such instruments can shed light on intriguing facets like patterns of movement, accessibility to resources, and the frequency of shelter visits.

Appreciating the complex dimensions of homelessness, there's a visible drift towards amalgamating diverse research techniques. This fusion of qualitative and quantitative data, which marries personal stories with empirical models, offers researchers a canvas that captures the phenomenon's vastness and its intricate details.

A pivotal shift in recent times is the inclination to engage homeless individuals beyond mere subjects of study. By welcoming them as proactive contributors to the research narrative, a more anchored and compassionate methodology emerges. The insights, lived experiences, and unique perspectives of those enduring homelessness make the research more attuned to the genuine challenges and requirements at the grassroots level.

In today's interconnected digital ecosystem, even homeless individuals leave behind subtle electronic traces. Be it interactions on online platforms or using computers in public libraries, there exists a vast reservoir of digital imprints. By harnessing the might of big data analytics paired with cutting-edge algorithmic designs, discernible patterns and service gaps come to the fore.

Another transformative stride in homelessness research is the birth of platforms facilitating instantaneous data gathering. Whether it's service professionals, volunteers, or the broader public, real-time logging of encounters, observations, or support provided, paints a lively and perpetually refreshed picture of the scenario.

And as we march ahead with these research advancements, the moral compass guiding them remains paramount. There's an intensified focus on ensuring research endeavors steer clear of practices that could be perceived as intrusive, opportunistic, or triggering past traumas. The accentuation on trauma-informed methodologies underscores the commitment to uphold the mental and emotional sanctity of participants, cherishing their inherent dignity and autonomy throughout the investigative journey.

This metamorphosis in research techniques is a testament to the broader evolution in our comprehension of homelessness. With the sharpening of tools and the broadening of perspectives, the aspiration remains unaltered: to unveil truths that are both reflective of reality and potent in their ability to guide actions, steering us towards an epoch where homelessness is relegated to history's annals.

Data Gaps and the Importance of Longitudinal Studies

In any research field, understanding what we don't know is as crucial as understanding what we do. In the realm of homelessness research, there have been persistent data gaps that hinder a comprehensive grasp of the issue. Often, these gaps arise from challenges in capturing certain demographics, limited geographic scope, or constraints in research funding and resources. However, merely identifying these gaps isn't enough; there's a pressing need to address them to ensure that policies and interventions are grounded in reality.

One significant gap is the 'hidden homeless'—individuals who might be couch surfing, temporarily staying with friends or family, or living in cars. Their transient nature and avoidance of official shelters or services make them challenging to count and study. Yet, their experiences, challenges, and needs might differ significantly from those who are visibly homeless or accessing shelter services.

Another notable data gap pertains to rural homelessness. Much of the research and media attention focuses on urban areas, but homelessness in rural regions, while perhaps less visible, is no less severe. The dynamics, causes, and solutions might differ in these areas, necessitating dedicated studies and interventions.

Enter longitudinal studies. These are not merely snapshots but extended narratives that trace the trajectories of homeless individuals over time. By repeatedly observing or surveying the same participants over extended periods, researchers can gather insights into the patterns, causes, and outcomes of homelessness. This temporal dimension is invaluable in understanding the cyclical nature of homelessness, the efficacy of interventions, and the long-term impacts on health, well-being, and socio-economic status.

Longitudinal studies also enable the identification of risk factors and early warning signs, allowing for timely interventions. They shed light on the transition points—what factors contribute to someone moving from temporary to chronic homelessness, or conversely, what aids in transitioning from homelessness to stable housing.

These studies hold the potential to challenge or confirm widely held beliefs. For instance, there's a prevailing notion that providing housing is the end goal. However, through longitudinal observation, it might emerge that while housing is crucial, other concurrent support systems, be it counseling, job training, or community integration, are equally pivotal for long-term stability.

Incorporating the insights from longitudinal studies, researchers, policymakers, and service providers can craft more informed, nuanced, and adaptive strategies. By filling the data gaps and understanding the evolving journey of homeless individuals, the goal of not just alleviating but eliminating homelessness comes into sharper focus.

Policy Impact Analysis: Assessing the Real-World Impact of Policies

Understanding the nuances of homelessness is one thing; assessing how policies play out in real-world scenarios is another critical aspect. Policies, while designed with good intentions, might have unforeseen consequences, or might not achieve their intended outcomes. That's where policy impact analysis comes into play. It's not about intentions, but outcomes.

At the heart of policy impact analysis is the question: "What difference did this policy make?" For researchers and policymakers, this question isn't just rhetorical. It necessitates a deep dive into data, field observations, and stakeholder feedback.

There's a need to establish a baseline — understanding the state of homelessness before the policy's implementation. This provides a reference point against which future observations can be compared. With this in place, researchers monitor various indicators over time, such as the number of people experiencing homelessness, the duration of homelessness, the health outcomes of those affected, and more.

A robust policy impact analysis doesn't stop at quantitative metrics. Qualitative insights, often gathered through interviews, focus groups, or participatory observations, provide a richer understanding. They capture the lived experiences of those affected by the policy, providing insights into aspects like the perceived adequacy of support services, the psychological impact of interventions, or the challenges still unaddressed.

An essential aspect of this analysis is understanding the differential impact. It recognizes that policies might not affect all sections of the population uniformly. For instance, an intervention aimed at assisting homeless families might have varying outcomes for single parents, large families, or those with special needs children. By pinpointing these differences, policies can be refined and tailored more effectively.

Another crucial component is the feedback loop. Policy impact analysis isn't a one-off process but an ongoing one. As data and insights emerge, they should feed back into the policymaking process, allowing for iterative improvements. This dynamic approach ensures that policies remain adaptive and responsive to the evolving landscape of homelessness.

Policy impact analysis serves a dual purpose. It holds policymakers accountable, ensuring that well-intentioned strategies translate into meaningful, tangible outcomes. Simultaneously, it provides a roadmap, guiding refinements and innovations, ensuring that efforts to combat homelessness remain grounded, effective, and humane.

Forecasting and Simulation Models: Predicting Future Trends

Forecasting and simulation models serve as powerful tools in understanding and projecting the trajectory of homelessness. As the landscape of homelessness evolves, influenced by socioeconomic factors, policy changes, and unforeseen events like pandemics or economic downturns, having an anticipatory approach becomes paramount.

In homelessness research, forecasting uses statistical techniques and data trends to predict future outcomes based on current and past data. For instance, by analyzing employment rates, housing costs, and social safety net policies, researchers can forecast potential spikes or decreases in homelessness. Such predictions are invaluable for policymakers and service providers, allowing them to allocate resources more efficiently and prepare for forthcoming challenges.

Simulation models, meanwhile, are more intricate. These models create a virtual environment that mimics real-world scenarios. Within this environment, researchers can modify variables to observe how they influence homelessness. For example, a simulation might explore how changes in minimum wage rates, housing policies, or mental health services availability might impact the rates of homelessness over a decade.

The power of forecasting and simulation models lies not only in their capacity to predict but also in the transformative benefits they offer to various stakeholders. Here's an exploration of these benefits:

Proactivity over Reactivity

One of the most substantial advantages these models bring is the shift in perspective. In many areas of social intervention, responses tend to be reactive, addressing challenges only after they've manifested. However, with accurate forecasting, stakeholders can pivot from this reactive stance. By gaining foresight into potential future trends, communities, organizations, and governments can anticipate challenges before they escalate. This proactive approach enables them to not only mitigate potential crises but also implement preventive measures, curbing the onset of issues before they burgeon. In the context of homelessness, such a shift could translate to the timely creation of shelters or resource centers in areas predicted to face increased homelessness or proactively boosting mental health support in regions foreseeing an economic downturn.

Resource Optimization

Resources, be it funding, manpower, or infrastructure, are often finite. Knowing where they are needed the most can significantly amplify the impact. Forecasting and simulation models offer a lens into potential areas of concern. By identifying potential hotspots of homelessness or zones that might face a significant strain in the future, governments and organizations can direct their resources with precision. Similarly, by understanding which demographics—whether based on age, race, or economic status—might be most vulnerable, targeted interventions can be designed, ensuring that help reaches those who need it the most.

Scenario Analysis

The future, with all its uncertainties, presents a plethora of possibilities. Simulation models, especially, empower researchers to venture into this realm of possibilities, allowing them to test out various "what if" scenarios. What if there's a sudden surge in rental prices? What if there's a cut in funding for mental health services? By modeling these scenarios, researchers can gain invaluable insights into potential outcomes. They can identify which interventions could prove most beneficial or detect policies that might inadvertently escalate homelessness rates. This process, akin to a sandbox experimentation in a controlled environment, not only aids in informed decision-making but also minimizes unforeseen negative repercussions.

Adaptive Policymaking

The landscape of homelessness is dynamic, influenced by a myriad of factors ranging from economic trends to societal shifts. Rigid policies, designed without a mechanism for adaptation, can quickly become obsolete or, worse, counterproductive. As forecasts and simulations shed light on potential trajectories, they usher in a new era of adaptive policymaking. Policymakers, equipped with insights from these models, can design policies that are not set in stone but are fluid, adapting to the changing landscape. These policies can have built-in review mechanisms or triggers that initiate revisions, ensuring they stay attuned to the evolving needs and challenges. This dynamic approach ensures that policies remain not just relevant but also effective in their mission to combat homelessness.

Together, these benefits underscore the transformative potential of forecasting and simulation models. They represent more than mere tools; they are catalysts that can drive meaningful, sustained change in the fight against homelessness. While these models offer valuable insights, they are not without limitations. The accuracy of forecasts and simulations is contingent upon the quality and completeness of the data they're based on. They also operate on assumptions, which, if incorrect, can skew outcomes. Thus, while they are instrumental in guiding decisions, they should be used in tandem with other research methodologies and continuously refined as new data becomes available.

Forecasting and simulation models represent a blend of art and science. They harness the power of data and technology to envisage potential futures, equipping stakeholders with the knowledge to shape a world where homelessness is a challenge of the past.

Chapter 9: The Path Forward

As we reflect upon the intricate web of factors and influences that contribute to the global challenge of homelessness, it becomes abundantly clear that there is no single solution, no magic wand to wave that will make the issue vanish overnight. Instead, the journey towards a world where homelessness is a relic of the past demands the weaving together of innovation, ethics, collaboration, and an unwavering commitment to humanity. This chapter delves deep into the fabric of that journey, unraveling the threads of progress and potential that lie ahead.

Building ethical, sustainable, and responsible innovation frameworks is more than just a strategic imperative; it is a moral one. In a world brimming with technological advancements and new-age solutions, it's tempting to be seduced by the allure of quick fixes. Yet, the challenge of homelessness, steeped as it is in historical, socio-economic, and human contexts, demands that we proceed with caution, ensuring that our strategies are as humane as they are innovative. This means that any technological or policy-driven solution must be evaluated not just for its efficacy but also for its ethical implications. Will it inadvertently marginalize certain communities? Does it uphold the dignity of the individuals it aims to serve?

The scale and complexity of homelessness underline the importance of collaboration and knowledge sharing. No single entity, be it a government, an NGO, or a community group, can tackle this issue in isolation. The insights from one region can offer invaluable lessons for another; the failures and successes of one initiative can illuminate the path for subsequent endeavors. By fostering an environment where knowledge flows freely, where collaborations are nurtured, and where every stakeholder, big or small, has a voice, we can accelerate our progress exponentially.

At the heart of all these efforts lies a fundamental principle: emphasizing humanity and ethics in every step. The individuals facing homelessness are not mere statistics; they are people with dreams, aspirations, fears, and hopes. Every policy, every innovation, every research study must be approached with this understanding. Only by placing humanity at the center of our efforts can we hope to craft solutions that are not just effective but also compassionate.

Building Ethical, Sustainable, and Responsible Innovation Frameworks

In today's rapidly evolving technological landscape, the solutions to many of society's challenges often seem to lie in the next big innovation. From artificial intelligence to blockchain, digital interventions are heralded as the panacea for a myriad of issues. However, when it comes to addressing the multifaceted challenge of homelessness, it is crucial to ensure that our innovations, while promising, are rooted in principles of ethics, sustainability, and responsibility.

An Ethical Innovation Framework (EIF)

An (EIF) champions the intrinsic worth and dignity of every human being. This principle, deep-rooted in our shared humanity, becomes especially pertinent when crafting solutions for some of society's most vulnerable members. In the context of homelessness, any intervention, be it technological or policy-driven, should not merely be about alleviating immediate distress but must aspire to holistically uplift the quality of life for these individuals. This upliftment is a multi-dimensional endeavor, encompassing not only their physical needs but also their emotional, psychological, and social well-being.

In the age of digital transformation, technology plays a pivotal role in devising solutions for homelessness. Digital platforms, with their vast reach and efficiency, have the potential to reshape traditional systems, making them more responsive and inclusive. Imagine a digital tool that simplifies the process of shelter registration, reducing wait times and ensuring that a homeless individual finds a safe space at the earliest. Or consider a platform that intelligently allocates resources based on real-time data, ensuring that food, medical supplies, or other essentials reach those in dire need promptly.

With the immense power of technology comes the pressing responsibility to wield it with caution and conscience. In the rush to innovate, the personal rights and autonomy of homeless individuals should never be overshadowed.

For example, while collecting data can aid in crafting tailored solutions, the privacy of these individuals remains paramount. Their personal data, which they often share in trust and hope, can be a goldmine for businesses, advertisers, or even malicious actors. Ensuring robust data protection measures is not just about legal compliance; it's a moral imperative. The commodification or misuse of this data, without explicit consent, is not only a breach of trust but a stark violation of the ethical standards we must uphold.

The process of innovation should actively involve seeking feedback from the homeless community. Too often, well-intentioned solutions miss the mark because they're not rooted in the lived experiences of those they aim to serve. By integrating their insights and concerns, especially concerning the use of personal data and technology, we can foster innovations that are not only effective but also deeply respectful and humane. In essence, an ethical innovation framework prioritizes the individual over the innovation, ensuring that every step taken is in service of dignity, respect, and holistic well-being.

Sustainability

As a concept, sustainability goes beyond short-term fixes; it's a commitment to forge lasting, impactful change. In the context of addressing homelessness, sustainability isn't merely about ensuring an individual has shelter for a night, but it's about systematically dismantling the structures that perpetuate homelessness and building robust systems that prevent its recurrence. The ultimate aim of sustainable interventions is to ensure that each solution, once implemented, creates a ripple effect of positive change that outlasts the immediate intervention.

Take, for instance, the example of transitional shelters. These establishments, vital as they are, primarily address the acute phase of homelessness. They offer a haven, a respite from the immediate dangers of the streets. However, the larger challenge remains: How do we ensure that an individual, once out of the transitional shelter, doesn't find themselves back on the streets in a few months or years? This is where the true essence of sustainability comes into play.

A sustainable approach would look at the entire ecosystem surrounding homelessness. It would delve into the root causes, such as job loss, medical emergencies, or lack of affordable housing, and strategize on ways to mitigate them. It's about recognizing that while shelters are essential, the real work lies in ensuring accessible education, job training, mental health support, and affordable housing. Each of these facets, when bolstered, acts as a safeguard against the cycle of recurring homelessness.

Sustainable interventions advocate for proactive rather than reactive measures. Instead of waiting for individuals to seek help, sustainable systems actively identify those at risk and provide timely interventions. This could mean counseling services for those undergoing severe financial strain, rent subsidies for families on the brink of eviction, or skill training for those whose jobs are becoming obsolete.

In a broader sense, sustainability also implies financial viability. Funds allocated towards homelessness interventions should be used judiciously, ensuring that each dollar spent maximizes impact. This might involve public-private partnerships, community-driven initiatives, or harnessing technology to drive efficiency. By ensuring that programs are both impactful and cost-effective, we lay the foundation for long-lasting solutions that not only serve the current generation but also future ones, ensuring that they inherit a world where homelessness is a relic of the past rather than a persistent challenge.

Responsibility in innovation necessitates a holistic approach to solution development. It means being accountable for the broader implications of an innovation, both intended and unintended.

If a city was to develop an app connecting homeless individuals with job opportunities, it would be responsible for ensuring that these jobs are safe, fair, and free from exploitation.

Involving the very individuals these innovations aim to serve in the ideation and execution phases can be transformative. Co-creating solutions with those who have experienced homelessness ensures that the strategies are grounded in real-life challenges and needs. This participatory approach can lead to solutions that are not only effective but also respectful, placing the lived experiences of the homeless at the heart of innovation.

It's worth noting that ethical, sustainable, and responsible innovation does not stand in opposition to efficiency or efficacy. Instead, it enhances them. By ensuring that innovations are rooted in these principles, we can craft solutions that stand the test of time, are embraced by communities, and most importantly, genuinely transform lives.

It's a journey of discovering that the most profound innovations often emerge when we merge cutting-edge technology with age-old values of empathy, respect, and solidarity.

The Need for Continued Collaboration and Knowledge Sharing

The complexities surrounding homelessness cannot be understated. It's an issue interwoven with numerous societal, economic, and personal factors, making it a challenge that can't be effectively addressed in isolation. The importance of collaboration and knowledge sharing emerges from this very intricacy, emphasizing that the path forward demands unified efforts from all sectors of society.

Governments, while equipped with the legislative and financial tools to instigate change, often grapple with the challenges of bureaucracy and policy limitations. Non-governmental organizations (NGOs) and community groups, on the other hand, possess grassroots knowledge and a deep understanding of localized issues but might lack the scale or resources to effect widespread change. Similarly, academic researchers can provide data-driven insights, but implementation remains a challenge. Corporates and businesses might have innovative solutions and funding but lack the community trust or understanding of ground realities. It becomes evident that each entity, while possessing strengths, also faces unique challenges.

Collaboration is the bridge that can connect these disparate entities, amplifying their strengths while mitigating their weaknesses. Joint ventures between governments and NGOs can combine legislative power with grassroots action. Partnerships between academic institutions and corporates can lead to research-driven, scalable solutions. The combined expertise, resources, and reach of these collaborations can pioneer holistic strategies that address homelessness at every level — from prevention to intervention and long-term support.

Collaboration isn't just about pooling resources. It's also about creating spaces for dialogue, understanding, and mutual learning. Knowledge sharing becomes paramount in this context. For instance, a city that has successfully reduced its homeless population through an innovative housing-first approach should share its learnings with other cities grappling with similar challenges. An NGO that has pioneered a community-driven rehabilitation program can offer insights to others looking to replicate their success elsewhere.

This symbiotic exchange of knowledge facilitates the growth of best practices, prevents the repetition of past mistakes, and accelerates the pace of positive change.

It fosters an environment where learnings from one corner of the world can inspire actions in another, creating a global community united in its commitment to eradicate homelessness. For such collaboration and knowledge sharing to be truly effective, certain prerequisites must be met. These include transparent communication, mutual respect, the establishment of common goals, and, above all, an unwavering commitment to place the well-being of the homeless population at the heart of every action. By doing so, we can harness the collective strength of diverse stakeholders and journey forward, with hope and determination, towards a world where everyone has a place to call home. For collaboration and knowledge sharing to genuinely bear fruit, it's essential to delve into the foundational elements that ensure effective cooperation among varied stakeholders.

Transparent Communication

At its core, transparent communication means that all parties involved share information openly, without hidden agendas. This is paramount, as the complexities of homelessness often require swift decisions and adaptability. If an NGO has reservations about a particular policy's effectiveness, it should communicate them. If a government body is constrained by budgetary limits, this needs to be conveyed. Transparent communication fosters trust, and with trust, collaborations can navigate the inevitable challenges they will encounter.

Mutual Respect

Each stakeholder, from community organizers to policymakers, plays a unique role in addressing homelessness. Recognizing the value that each party brings to the table is crucial. Mutual respect ensures that different perspectives are considered, leading to more holistic solutions. It's this respect that paves the way for genuine listening, where feedback is not just heard but integrated into strategies and actions.

Establishment of Common Goals

While each entity might have its specific objectives — be it research, policy implementation, or direct intervention — it's essential that there's alignment on overarching goals. A shared vision, such as the commitment to reduce homelessness by a certain percentage over a defined period, can act as a north star, guiding collaborative efforts and ensuring that individual actions contribute to the collective objective.

Commitment to the Well-being of the Homeless

Beyond strategies, metrics, and collaborations lies the heart of the matter: the individuals experiencing homelessness. Every decision, no matter how strategic or well-intentioned, must be evaluated against its impact on this vulnerable population. Are we enhancing their dignity? Are we offering them not just shelter but a pathway to stability and hope? This unwavering commitment is the litmus test for all collaborative actions.

When these foundational principles are embedded in collaborative efforts, they transcend mere transactional interactions, evolving into transformative partnerships. Such collaborations don't just share resources; they share dreams of a world where the blight of homelessness is a thing of the past. It's through this united front, where each stakeholder brings its strengths and learns from its weaknesses, that we can inch closer to a reality where every individual, regardless of their circumstances, has the assurance of a safe, dignified, and stable living environment. In this collective endeavor, the whole truly becomes greater than the sum of its parts.

Emphasizing Humanity and Ethics in Every Step

At the core of our quest to address homelessness lies an imperative far greater than any technological advancement, policy, or strategy: the unwavering emphasis on humanity and ethics. As we advance in our methods, evolve our systems, and harness unprecedented collaborations, it is essential to remember that at the center of our efforts are people—each with their dreams, aspirations, fears, and vulnerabilities.

Our commitment to humanity necessitates that we continually prioritize the dignity, rights, and well-being of those experiencing homelessness. This means that we must not only provide shelter but also foster environments where individuals can heal, grow, and reclaim their autonomy. It means that we must actively challenge any form of stigmatization or discrimination and empower individuals with choices and voices in decisions that affect them.

Ethics, intertwined with our commitment to humanity, serves as our moral compass. It reminds us to be vigilant about the implications of our actions and interventions, ensuring that they do not inadvertently harm or marginalize those we aim to help. As we innovate and explore new solutions, our ethical considerations must weigh the potential benefits against any risks, always erring on the side of preserving individual rights and dignity.

Our dedication to ethics calls for transparency and accountability in all our endeavors. It demands that we critically evaluate our approaches, rectify mistakes, and celebrate successes with humility. It is this ethical foundation that will foster trust among stakeholders, ensuring that the journey forward is cohesive and principled.

As we navigate the complexities of addressing homelessness and chart our path forward, our compass must be calibrated by these twin pillars of humanity and ethics. They remind us that while our goal is to eradicate homelessness, our broader mission is to create a world that respects, values, and uplifts every individual. Let this be the legacy of our collective efforts: a world where compassion, dignity, and justice are not mere ideals but lived realities for all.

As we draw to a close on our exploration of homelessness, it is both a moment of reflection and anticipation. The myriad facets of homelessness, ranging from its underlying causes to the multiplicity of its solutions, have been unwrapped layer by layer, revealing the depth and breadth of an issue that touches every corner of our global community. The intricate tapestry we've woven together is a testament to the complexity of the challenge, but also to the potential for transformative change. It underscores the imperative to transition from understanding to action, from sympathy to solidarity, and from isolation to collective endeavor.

We delved deep into the multidimensional facets of homelessness, uncovering the intricate interplay of socio-economic, political, and personal factors that lead individuals and families to experience housing instability. From the foundational understanding of homelessness and its myriad classifications, we traversed the complex terrains of prevention, intervention, and proactive measures. We learned that education, employment, and healthcare are not just basic human rights, but powerful protective barriers against the descent into homelessness.

Our journey also took us to the crossroads of homelessness and social justice, revealing the disproportionate impact of homelessness on marginalized communities—from indigenous populations and LGBTQ+ individuals to migrants and refugees. These intersections highlighted the compounded vulnerabilities certain demographics face and emphasized the importance of targeted, culturally sensitive interventions.

In assessing the latest research trends, we appreciated the ever-evolving methodologies that researchers employ, from field studies to virtual surveys. We delved into the importance of bridging data gaps, recognizing the unparalleled insights longitudinal studies offer and the weight of policy impact analyses. Through forecasting and simulation models, we glimpsed the potential trajectories of homelessness, understanding that predictive insights are crucial tools in our proactive arsenal.

The discourse on collaboration and knowledge sharing underscored the value of collective effort. We recognized that silos, whether in research, policymaking, or intervention, can impede progress. But by fostering an environment of mutual respect, shared goals, and transparent communication, we stand a better chance of making impactful strides.

Lastly, we were reminded that at the core of all these discussions, analyses, and strategies is the human element. Every statistic represents a life, every policy impacts a community, and every intervention has the potential to change a person's trajectory. As we forge ahead, our actions must be rooted in empathy, respect, and a deep-seated commitment to upholding the dignity of every individual.

As we close this chapter, it's evident that our learning is both vast and deep, but it's also a living body of knowledge. The landscape of homelessness, shaped by socio-political changes, economic fluctuations, and evolving societal norms, will continue to change. But armed with the insights from our exploration, we are better equipped to adapt, respond, and most importantly, make a difference.

The Journey Ahead: Challenges, Hopes, and the Collective Vision

The road to eradicating homelessness is a journey fraught with a mosaic of intricacies. It's a labyrinth where each turn presents a fresh challenge, sometimes anticipated, often unexpected.

These challenges, however, are not mere impediments; they are reminders of the gravity and scale of the mission ahead. They echo the voices of those still seeking shelter, of children born into transiency, and of families fractured by the overwhelming weight of uncertainty.

The complexity of the issue is mirrored in its multifaceted causes—economic downturns, societal inequalities, systemic failures, and personal tragedies—all converging to push individuals to the peripheries of society. The enormity of the task at hand can sometimes seem daunting, casting shadows of doubt and despondency.

Intertwined with these formidable challenges is an undying spirit of hope and resilience. Each challenge, in its essence, is an invitation—a call to think differently, to embrace innovative solutions, and to foster partnerships that transcend traditional boundaries. The adversity faced paves the way for community-driven collaborations, technological advancements, and policy reforms. It nudges us towards reimagining conventional norms and reconstructing societal frameworks.

This journey, while challenging, is also emblematic of a collective aspiration—a vision deeply embedded in the human spirit. It's a vision of a world devoid of the agony of homelessness, where streets no longer serve as makeshift homes and where every child, adult, and elder has a secure haven. A world sculpted by our collective endeavors, where compassion, justice, and solidarity shape the very foundation of our societies.

As we traverse this journey, we are not merely guided by the North Star of eradicating homelessness but inspired by the transformative potential of our shared human experience. The voyage ahead is one of unity and unwavering commitment, and it beckons us to rise, together, towards a horizon filled with promise and hope.

From Awareness to Action: A Call to Every Reader

This exploration isn't just a testament to knowledge but a clarion call to each reader. The baton is now in your hands. Awareness, while powerful, is but the first step. It is the ensuing action, catalyzed by this awareness, that brings about tangible change. Whether you are a policymaker, an advocate, a researcher, or a concerned citizen, the narrative of homelessness can be reshaped by your interventions. Embrace the role you can play, no matter how big or small, for in the chorus of collective action, every voice matters. Together, we can transition from understanding the plight of the homeless to forging a world where homelessness is a thing of the past.

Delving into the nuances of homelessness has been more than just an academic endeavor; it's a revelation, a compelling narrative that interweaves stories of despair and hope, of challenges met and battles still raging. And now, as we reach the culmination of this journey, the onus shifts. It rests not just on the shoulders of the few but on the collective conscience of every reader.

True, awareness is the dawn of change. It illuminates the corners of our understanding, shedding light on areas previously overlooked. But merely being aware, while crucial, is akin to standing at the edge of a vast expanse, contemplating the journey but not embarking upon it. It's the momentum of action, fueled by this newfound awareness, that propels us forward, transforming intent into impact.

Each one of you, dear readers, is poised at a unique vantage point. Whether you helm the corridors of power, champion causes in community alleys, delve into the intricacies of research, or simply hold the earnest desire to make a difference, you possess the potential to influence the trajectory of homelessness. Realize that every effort counts. A researcher's findings might pave the way for policy reforms; a concerned citizen's grassroots initiative can light up lives, and an advocate's fervor can mobilize masses.

In this grand tapestry of change, every thread, every gesture, every voice has its place and purpose. Let's not be content with mere cognizance. Let's rise, galvanized by the stories we've encountered, the lessons we've gleaned, and the shared vision we hold. Let our collective endeavors be the winds of change, steering us closer to a world where the term 'homeless' finds no resonance, where every individual has a rightful place to call their own.

As we close the pages of this book, let's not consider it an end, but rather a beginning—a launching point into a world of action, understanding, and compassion. Throughout these chapters, we've embarked on a profound journey into the complexities of homelessness, unraveling its intricacies and seeking solutions. Yet, the true essence of this journey is not just in the details, statistics, or strategies discussed but in the shared humanity that binds us all.

Homelessness, in many ways, serves as a mirror to society, reflecting both our shortcomings and our potential. It is a poignant reminder of the vulnerabilities we all could face, a testament to the impermanence of circumstance. But more than that, it underscores the strength of the human spirit, the resilience of those who endure, and the boundless compassion of those who step forward to help.

My sincerest hope is that this exploration resonates with you, not just as information, but as an inspiration—a catalyst that ignites a flame of action, no matter how small. Remember, every gesture, every initiative, and every voice can ripple out, creating waves of change.

And so, dear reader, as you return to the world outside these pages, carry with you the stories, insights, and imperatives. Let them be a compass guiding your endeavors, and let empathy be your constant companion. As we step forward, may we all remain united in our pursuit of a world where the sanctity of 'home' is a right, not a privilege.

Wishing you a journey filled with purpose, understanding, and transformative impact. Let's co-create a world where love, compassion, and shelter abound for all.

References

Chapter 1

Burt, M. R., Aron, L. Y., Douglas, T., Valente, J., Lee, E., & Iwen, B. (1999). Homelessness: Programs and the people they serve. Urban Institute.

Culhane, D. P., & Metraux, S. (2008). Rearranging the deck chairs or reallocating the lifeboats? Homelessness assistance and its alternatives. Journal of the American Planning Association, 74(1), 111-121.

Desmond, M. (2016). Evicted: Poverty and profit in the American city. Crown.

Edelman, P. (2017). Not a crime to be poor: The criminalization of poverty in America. The New Press.

Gaetz, S., Dej, E., Richter, T., & Redman, M. (2016). The state of homelessness in Canada 2016. Canadian Observatory on Homelessness Press.

Hopper, K., Jost, J., Hay, T., Welber, S., & Haugland, G. (1997). Homelessness, severe mental illness, and the institutional circuit. Psychiatric Services, 48(5), 659-665.

Kuhn, R., & Culhane, D. P. (1998). Applying cluster analysis to test a typology of homelessness by pattern of shelter utilization: Results from the analysis of administrative data. American Journal of Community Psychology, 26(2), 207-232.

National Alliance to End Homelessness. (2012). The state of homelessness in America. NAEH.

Parsell, C., Petersen, M., & Culhane, D. P. (Eds.). (2017). Cost offsets of supportive housing: Evidence for social work. British Journal of Social Work, 47(5), 1534-1553.

Quigley, J. M., Raphael, S., & Smolensky, E. (2001). Homeless in America, homeless in California. Review of Economics and Statistics, 83(1), 37-51.

Rossi, P. H. (1990). The old homeless and the new homeless in historical perspective. American Psychologist, 45(8), 954.

Tsemberis, S., & Eisenberg, R. F. (2000). Pathways to housing: Supported housing for street-dwelling homeless individuals with psychiatric disabilities. Psychiatric Services, 51(4), 487-493.

Tsai, J., & Rosenheck, R. A. (2015). Risk factors for homelessness among US veterans. Epidemiologic Reviews, 37(1), 177-195.

Wasserman, J. A., & Clair, J. M. (2010). At Home on the Street: People, Poverty, and a Hidden Culture of Homelessness. Lynne Rienner Publishers.

Chapter 2

Barry, C. L., McGinty, E. E., Pescosolido, B. A., & Goldman, H. H. (2014). Stigma, discrimination, treatment effectiveness, and policy: Public views about drug addiction and mental illness. Psychiatric Services, 65(10), 1269-1272.

Charette, R. N. (2013). Big data, big challenges. IEEE Spectrum, 50(4), 44-49.

Cukier, K., & Mayer-Schoenberger, V. (2013). The rise of big data: How it's changing the way we think about the world. Foreign Affairs, 92(3), 28.

De Mauro, A., Greco, M., & Grimaldi, M. (2016). A formal definition of big data based on its essential features. Library Review, 65(3), 122-135.

Duan, L., & Xu, L. (2012). Business intelligence for enterprise systems: A survey. IEEE Transactions on Industrial Informatics, 8(3), 679-687.

Ferris, L., & Kahn, D. (2018). Artificial Intelligence in public health surveillance: Opportunities and challenges. Journal of Public Health Management and Practice, 24(3), 294-298.

Greenhalgh, T., & Russell, J. (2010). Why do evaluations of eHealth programs fail? An alternative set of guiding principles. PloS Medicine, 7(11), e1000360.

Kitchin, R. (2014). The data revolution: big data, open data, data infrastructures and their consequences. Sage.

Mittelstadt, B. D., Allo, P., Taddeo, M., Wachter, S., & Floridi, L. (2016). The ethics of algorithms: Mapping the debate. Big Data & Society, 3(2), 205395171667967.

O'Neil, C. (2016). Weapons of math destruction: How big data increases inequality and threatens democracy. Crown.

Pascale, R., Sternin, J., & Sternin, M. (2010). The power of positive deviance: How unlikely innovators solve the world's toughest problems. Harvard Business Press.

Patel, V. L., Shortliffe, E. H., Stefanelli, M., Szolovits, P., Berthold, M. R., Bellazzi, R., & Abu-Hanna, A. (2009). The coming of age of artificial intelligence in medicine. Artificial Intelligence in Medicine, 46(1), 5-17.

Richards, N. M., & King, J. H. (2013). Big data ethics. Wake Forest Law Review, 49, 393.

Tene, O., & Polonetsky, J. (2012). Big data for all: Privacy and user control in the age of analytics. Northwestern Journal of Technology and Intellectual Property, 11, xxvii.

Chapter 3

Culhane, D. P., Metraux, S., & Hadley, T. (2002). Public service reductions associated with placement of homeless persons with severe mental illness in supportive housing. Housing Policy Debate, 13(1), 107-163.

Gaetz, S. (2013). The Housing First model: Immediate access to permanent housing and support. Homeless Hub Research Paper Series.

Greenwood, R. M., Stefancic, A., Tsemberis, S., & Busch-Geertsema, V. (2013). Implementations of Housing First in Europe: Successes and challenges in maintaining model fidelity. American Journal of Psychiatric Rehabilitation, 16(4), 290-312.

Gulcur, L., Stefancic, A., Shinn, M., Tsemberis, S., & Fischer, S. N. (2003). Housing, hospitalization, and cost outcomes for homeless individuals with psychiatric disabilities participating in continuum of care and housing first programmes. Journal of Community & Applied Social Psychology, 13(2), 171-186.

Kresky-Wolff, M., Larson, M. J., O'Brien, R. W., & McGraw, S. A. (2010). Supportive housing approaches in the Collaborative Initiative to Help End Chronic Homelessness (CICH). The Journal of Behavioral Health Services & Research, 37(2), 213-225.

Padgett, D. K., Stanhope, V., Henwood, B. F., & Stefancic, A. (2011). Substance use outcomes among homeless clients with serious mental illness: Comparing Housing First with Treatment First programs. Community Mental Health Journal, 47(2), 227-232.

Pleace, N. (2011). The ambiguities, limits and risks of Housing First from a European perspective. European Journal of Homelessness, 5(2), 113-127.

Quilgars, D., & Pleace, N. (2016). Housing First and social integration: A realistic aim? Social Inclusion, 4(4), 5-15.

Rog, D. J., Marshall, T., Dougherty, R. H., George, P., Daniels, A. S., Ghose, S. S., & Delphin-Rittmon, M. E. (2014). Permanent supportive housing: Assessing the evidence. Psychiatric Services, 65(3), 287-294.

Tsemberis, S., Gulcur, L., & Nakae, M. (2004). Housing First, consumer choice, and harm reduction for homeless individuals with a dual diagnosis. American Journal of Public Health, 94(4), 651-656.
Waegemakers Schiff, J., & Rook, J. (2012). Housing First - Where is the evidence? Homeless Hub Research Paper Series.

Watson, D. P., Orwat, J., Wagner, D. E., Shuman, V., & Tolliver, R. (2013). The Housing First model (HFM) Fidelity Index: Designing and testing a tool for measuring integrity of housing programs that serve active substance users. Substance Abuse Treatment, Prevention, and Policy, 8(1), 16.

Chapter 4

Aldrich, R. P. (2015). Engaging the homeless: Participatory approaches and community decision-making. New York: Routledge.

Bartels, L., & Lupton, C. (2017). Public-private partnerships in urban areas: Benefits and pitfalls. Urban Studies Journal, 54(12), 2763-2782.

Collins, S. E., Malone, D. K., & Larimer, M. E. (2012). Motivating homeless youth: Advancing decision-making processes through community engagement. Community Mental Health Journal, 48(4), 457-465.

Fitzgerald, J., & Rose, K. (2013). Public-private partnerships: Their role in addressing homelessness. Journal of Housing and Social Equity, 11(2), 98-110.

Gardner, D. L. (2016). Collaborative solutions for homelessness: Lessons from leading cities. Urban Policy Review, 29(1), 24-37.

Harper, A. J., & Jones, M. (2014). Engaging the marginalized: Strategies and challenges in participatory design. Design Issues, 30(3), 23-34.

Mitchell, R. L., & Rankin, J. H. (2019). Successful collaborations in homelessness initiatives: A case study approach. Journal of Urban Affairs, 41(7), 985-1001.

Perez, V. L., & Thompson, E. (2018). Building partnerships: Best practices for public-private collaborations. Public Management Review, 20(8), 1165-1184.

Robinson, W. S. (2017). Homeless voices: The importance of involving those affected in policy decisions and interventions. Social Inclusion, 5(3), 72-81.

Smith, J., & Horan, A. (2016). Stories of impact: The role of collaboration in solving urban homelessness. Urban Sociology Review, 15(2), 47-63.

Thompson, R. J., & Pollock, W. (2020). Engagement strategies for homeless populations: A qualitative exploration. Social Service Review, 94(1), 125-150.

Winslow, B. T., & Hopper, K. (2015). Community engagement and collaborative partnerships in addressing homelessness. Journal of Community Practice, 23(2), 256-274.

Chapter 5

Culhane, D. P., Metraux, S., & Byrne, T. (2011). A prevention-centered approach to homelessness assistance: A paradigm shift? Housing Policy Debate, 21(2), 295-312.

Desmond, M. (2016). Evicted: Poverty and profit in the American city. Broadway Books.

Edgar, B., & Meert, H. (2005). Fourth review of statistics on homelessness in Europe. European Observatory on Homelessness.

Fitzpatrick, S., & Stephens, M. (2007). An international review of homelessness and social housing policy. Department for Communities and Local Government.

Gaetz, S. (2013). Coming of age: Reimagining the response to youth homelessness in Canada. Homeless Hub Report Series.
Goering, P., Veldhuizen, S., Watson, A., Adair, C., Kopp, B.,

Latimer, E., & Ly, A. (2014). National At Home/Chez Soi Final Report. Mental Health Commission of Canada.

Hopper, K., Shinn, M., Laska, E., Meisner, M., & Wanderling, J. (2008). Estimating numbers of unsheltered homeless people through plant-capture and postcount survey methods. American Journal of Public Health, 98(8), 1438-1442.

Kuhn, R., & Culhane, D. P. (1998). Applying cluster analysis to test a typology of homelessness by pattern of shelter utilization: Results from the analysis of administrative data. American Journal of Community Psychology, 26(2), 207-232.

Markee, P. (1997). A right to shelter. Yale Law & Policy Review, 15(2), 365-383.

National Law Center on Homelessness & Poverty. (2011). Criminalizing crisis: The criminalization of homelessness in U.S. cities.

O'Flaherty, B. (2004). Making room: The economics of homelessness. Harvard University Press.

Parsell, C., & Parsell, M. (2012). Homelessness as a choice. Housing, Theory and Society, 29(4), 420-434.

Quigley, J. M., Raphael, S., & Smolensky, E. (2001). Homelessness in California. Public Policy Institute of California.

Rosenheck, R., Bassuk, E., & Salomon, A. (1999). Special populations of homeless Americans. Practical lessons: The 1998 National Symposium on Homelessness Research.

Somerville, P. (2013). Understanding homelessness. Housing, Theory and Society, 30(4), 384-415.

Tsemberis, S., Gulcur, L., & Nakae, M. (2004). Housing First, consumer choice, and harm reduction for homeless individuals with a dual diagnosis. American Journal of Public Health, 94(4), 651-656.

U.S. Department of Housing and Urban Development. (2015). The 2015 Annual Homeless Assessment Report (AHAR) to Congress.

Chapter 6

Aubry, T., Klodawsky, F., & Coulombe, D. (2012). Comparing the housing trajectories of different classes within a diverse homeless population. American Journal of Community Psychology, 49(1-2), 142-155.

Culhane, D. P., Metraux, S., & Hadley, T. (2002). Public service reductions associated with placement of homeless persons with severe mental illness in supportive housing. Housing Policy Debate, 13(1), 107-163.

Desmond, M. (2016). Evicted: Poverty and profit in the American city. Broadway Books.

Gaetz, S., & Dej, E. (2017). A new direction: A framework for homelessness prevention. Canadian Observatory on Homelessness Press.

Henwood, B. F., Derejko, K. S., Couture, J., & Padgett, D. K. (2015). Maslow and mental health recovery: A comparative study of homeless programs for adults with serious mental illness. Administration and Policy in Mental Health and Mental Health Services Research, 42(2), 220-228.

Kertesz, S. G., Crouch, K., Milby, J. B., Cusimano, R. E., & Schumacher, J. E. (2009). Housing First for homeless persons with active addiction: Are we overreaching? Milbank Quarterly, 87(2), 495-534.

Mackelprang, J. L., Qiu, Q., & Rivara, F. P. (2015). Predictors of functional limitation trajectories after injury in a nationally representative US older adult population. American journal of epidemiology, 181(7), 465-473.

Montgomery, A. E., Hill, L. L., Kane, V., & Culhane, D. P. (2013). Housing chronically homeless veterans: Evaluating the efficacy of a Housing First approach to HUD-VASH. Journal of Community Psychology, 41(4), 505-514.

Parsell, C., & Moutou, O. (2014). Supportive housing: Lessons from Australia about the suite of services required, and client characteristics that predict sustained tenancy. Australian Social Work, 67(2), 256-268.

Spellman, B., & Khadduri, J. (2020). Implementing rapid re-housing: A review of lessons from Pathways Home. Housing Policy Debate, 30(1), 178-192.

Tsemberis, S. (2010). Housing First: The pathways model to end homelessness for people with mental illness and addiction. Hazelden Publishing.

Watson, J. P., Crawley, J., Kane, D., & Lomax, D. (2019). Working together to address homelessness in rural communities. Journal of Rural Health, 35(4), 597-601.

Woodhall-Melnik, J. R., & Dunn, J. R. (2015). A systematic review of outcomes associated with participation in Housing First programs. Housing Studies, 31(3), 287-304.

Zlotnick, C., Tam, T., & Bradley, K. (2010). Long-term and chronic homelessness in homeless women and women with children. Social Work in Public Health, 25(5), 470-485.

Chapter 7

Bassuk, E. L., & Beardslee, W. R. (2014). Depression in homeless mothers: Addressing an unrecognized public health issue. American Journal of Orthopsychiatry, 84(1), 73-81.

Beijer, U., Wolf, A., & Fazel, S. (2012). Prevalence of tuberculosis, hepatitis C virus, and HIV in homeless people: a systematic review and meta-analysis. The Lancet Infectious Diseases, 12(11), 859-870.

Burt, M. R., Aron, L. Y., & Lee, E. (2001). Helping America's homeless: Emergency shelter or affordable housing? Urban Institute Press.

Cloke, P., May, J., & Johnsen, S. (2010). Swept up lives? Re-envisioning the homeless city. Wiley-Blackwell.

Culhane, D. P., Park, J. M., & Metraux, S. (2011). The patterns and costs of services use among homeless families. Journal of Community Psychology, 39(7), 815-825.

Desmond, M. (2016). Evicted: Poverty and profit in the American city. Broadway Books.

Echenberg, H., & Jensen, H. (2009). Defining and enumerating homelessness in Canada. Library of Parliament.

Gowan, T. (2010). Hobos, hustlers, and backsliders: Homeless in San Francisco. University of Minnesota Press.

Hopper, K., Jost, J., Hay, T., Welber, S., & Haugland, G. (1997). Homelessness, severe mental illness, and the institutional circuit. Psychiatric Services, 48(5), 659-665.

Johnsen, S., Cloke, P., & May, J. (2005). Day centres for homeless people: spaces of care or fear? Social & Cultural Geography, 6(6), 787-811.

Karabanow, J. (2004). Being young and homeless: Understanding how youth enter and exit street life. Peter Lang.

Larkin, H., Aykanian, A., & Streeter, C. L. (2019). Homelessness prevention: Shifting the narrative from ending to preventing homelessness. Journal of Social Distress and Homelessness, 28(1), 68-76.

Pleace, N., & Bretherton, J. (2017). What do we mean by Housing First? Categorising and critically assessing the Housing First movement from a European perspective. FEANTSA.

Rossi, P. H. (1990). The old homeless and the new homeless in historical perspective. American Psychologist, 45(8), 954-959.

Thistle, J. (2017). Indigenous definition of homelessness in Canada. Canadian Observatory on Homelessness Press.

Watson, D. P., Wagner, D. E., & Rivers, M. (2013). Understanding the critical ingredients for facilitating consumer change in Housing First programming: A case study approach. The Journal of Behavioral Health Services & Research, 40(2), 169-179.

Chapter 8

Benjaminsen, L., & Andrade, S. B. (2015). Testing a typology of homelessness across welfare regimes: Shelter use in Denmark and the USA. Housing Studies, 30(6), 858-876.

Busch-Geertsema, V., & Sahlin, I. (2007). The role of hostels and temporary accommodation. European Journal of Homelessness, 1, 67-93.

Culhane, D. P., & Metraux, S. (2008). Rearranging the deck chairs or reallocating the lifeboats? Homelessness assistance and its alternatives. Journal of the American Planning Association, 74(1), 111-121.

Fitzpatrick, S., Bramley, G., & Johnsen, S. (2013). Pathways into multiple exclusion homelessness in seven UK cities. Urban Studies, 50(1), 148-168.

Gaetz, S., Barr, C., Friesen, A., Harris, B., Hill, C., Kovacs-Burns, K., ... & Turner, A. (2013). Canadian definition of homelessness. Canadian Observatory on Homelessness Press.

Kuhn, R., & Culhane, D. P. (1998). Applying cluster analysis to test a typology of homelessness by pattern of shelter utilization: Results from the analysis of administrative data. American Journal of Community Psychology, 26(2), 207-232.

Lyon-Callo, V. (2008). Inequality, poverty, and neoliberal governance: Activist ethnography in the homeless sheltering industry. University of Toronto Press.

Parsell, C., & Parsell, M. (2012). Homelessness as a choice. Housing, Theory and Society, 29(4), 420-434.

Pleace, N. (2016). Exclusion by definition: The under-representation of women in European homelessness statistics. Women and Homelessness in Europe: Pathways, Services and Experiences, 105.

Snow, D. A., & Anderson, L. (1993). Down on their luck: A study of homeless street people. University of California Press. Somerville, P. (2013). Understanding homelessness. Housing, Theory and Society, 30(4), 384-415.

Speak, S., & Tipple, G. (2006). Perceptions, persecution and pity: The limitations of interventions for homelessness in developing countries. International Journal of Urban and Regional Research, 30(1), 172-188.

Toro, P. A. (2007). Toward an international understanding of homelessness. Journal of Social Issues, 63(3), 461-481.

Tsai, J., & Rosenheck, R. A. (2015). Risk factors for homelessness among US veterans. Epidemiologic Reviews, 37(1), 177-195.

Waegemakers Schiff, J., & Turner, A. (2014). Housing First in rural Canada: rural homelessness and housing first feasibility across 22 Canadian communities. Preventing and Reducing Homelessness in Canada, 1-20.

Watson, J., Crawley, J., & Kane, D. (2016). Social media and homelessness: understanding the lived experience through online narrative. New technology in the human services, 28(1), 36-53.

Williams, A. R., & Olfson, M. (2018). Homelessness and mental illness. The Oxford Handbook of Stigma, Discrimination, and Health, 287.

Wood, L., & Foster, S. (2014). Geographies of homelessness: An overview. Geographical Journal, 180(3), 194-198.

Chapter 9

Burt, M. R., & Cohen, B. E. (1989). America's homeless: Numbers, characteristics, and programs that serve them. Urban Institute Press.

Cnaan, R. A., Milofsky, C., & Wong, N. W. (2013). Innovations in the public and nonprofit sectors: A public solutions handbook. Routledge.

Davis, M. (1990). City of quartz: Excavating the future in Los Angeles. Verso.

Edgar, B., & Meert, H. (2006). Fourth review of statistics on homelessness in Europe. The ETHOS Definition of Homelessness. Brussels, FEANTSA.

Greene, S., & Schmiege, C. J. (1998). Homelessness prevention: Creating programs that work. Brunner/Mazel.

Johnson, G., & Chamberlain, C. (2008). From youth to adult homelessness. Australian Journal of Social Issues, 43(4), 563-582.

Kidder, D. P., Wolitski, R. J., Campsmith, M. L., & Nakamura, G. V. (2007). Health status, health care use, medication use, and medication adherence among homeless and housed people living with HIV/AIDS. American Journal of Public Health, 97(12), 2238-2245.

Lupton, D., & Seymour, W. (2000). Technology, selfhood and physical disability. Social Science & Medicine, 50(12), 1851-1862.

Manthorpe, J., & Martineau, S. (2008). Serious case reviews in adult safeguarding in England: An analysis of a sample of reports. British Journal of Social Work, 38(3), 564-584.

Reckwitz, A. (2002). Toward a theory of social practices: A development in culturalist theorizing. European Journal of Social Theory, 5(2), 243-263.

Wasserman, J. A., & Clair, J. M. (2010). At home on the street: People, poverty, and a hidden culture of homelessness. Lynne Rienner Publishers.

Chapter 10

Desmond, M. (2016). Evicted: Poverty and profit in the American city. Broadway Books.

Gaetz, S., Barr, C., Friesen, A., Harris, B., Hill, C., Kovacs-Burns, K., ... & Pauly, B. (2013). Canadian definition of homelessness. Canadian Observatory on Homelessness Press.

Hopper, K. (1991). Research for what? Making a difference with social science knowledge. Free Press.

Kuhn, R., & Culhane, D. P. (1998). Applying cluster analysis to test a typology of homelessness by pattern of shelter utilization: Results from the analysis of administrative data. American Journal of Community Psychology, 26(2), 207-232.

Shinn, M. (2010). Ending homelessness for families: The evidence for affordable housing. National Alliance to End Homelessness.